CITYSPOTS

SEVILLE

Nick Inman

Thomas Cook

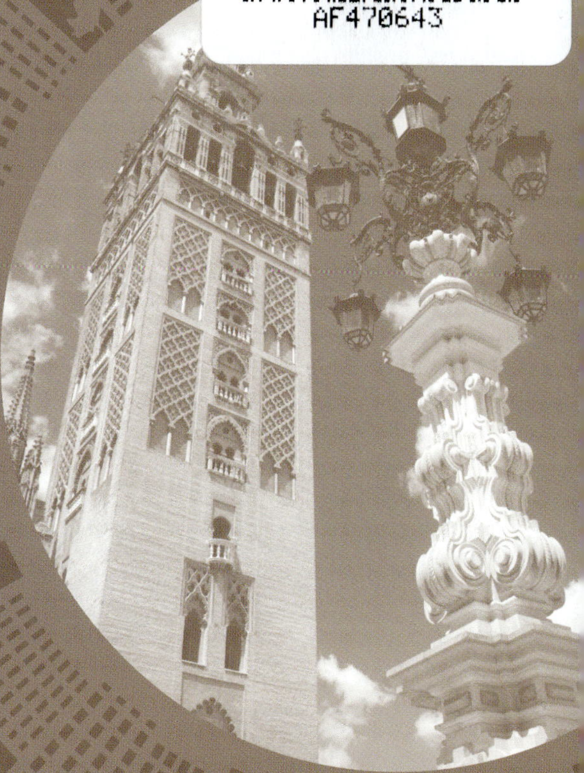

Written by Nick Inman
Updated by Sally Davies & Nadia Feddo

Published by Thomas Cook Publishing
A division of Thomas Cook Tour Operations Limited
Company registration No: 1450464 England
The Thomas Cook Business Park, 9 Coningsby Road
Peterborough PE3 8SB, United Kingdom
Email: books@thomascook.com, Tel: +44 (0)1733 416477
www.thomascookpublishing.com

Produced by The Content Works Ltd
Aston Court, Kingsmead Business Park, Frederick Place
High Wycombe, Bucks HP11 1LA
www.thecontentworks.com

Series design based on an original concept by Studio 183 Limited

ISBN: 978-1-84157-936-8

First edition © 2006 Thomas Cook Publishing
This second edition © 2008 Thomas Cook Publishing
Text © Thomas Cook Publishing
Maps © Thomas Cook Publishing/PCGraphics (UK) Limited
Transport map © Communicarta Limited

Series Editor: Kelly Anne Pipes
Project Editor: Linda Bass
Production/DTP: Steven Collins

Printed and bound in Spain by GraphyCems

Cover photography (Patio de los Embajadores) © Art Kowalsky/Alamy

CONTENTS

SYMBOLS KEY

The following symbols are used throughout this book:

ⓐ address ⓣ telephone ⓦ website address
🄾 opening times ❶ important

The following symbols are used on the maps:

𝒊 information office		points of interest
✈ airport	○	city
✚ hospital	○	large town
🛡 police station	○	small town
🚌 bus station	═	motorway
🚆 railway station	—	main road
✝ cathedral	—	minor road
❶ numbers denote featured	—	railway
cafés & restaurants		

Hotels and restaurants are graded by approximate price as follows:
£ budget price ££ mid-range price £££ expensive

Abbreviations used in addresses:
Av.   Avenida (Avenue)
C/   Calle (Street)
Pl.   Plaza (Square)

⬤ *The arches of the Alcázares*

INTRODUCING
Seville

Introduction

If any city can encapsulate the colour, sensuality, vitality and carefree spirit of southern Europe, it has to be Seville. It's a place that leaves few visitors cold. Rather, most of them feel compelled towards glowing superlatives. Camilo José Cela, Spain's Nobel Prize-winning novelist, declared it a city capable of inspiring even the dullest of poets. The travel writer Nina Epton, meanwhile, observed that 'the most abstemious of visitors feels inebriated in Seville'.

Spain's fourth-largest city and the capital of the region of Andalucia, it's the only city in the country to sit astride a major river, the great, green-flowing Guadalquivir River, 60 navigable kilometres (37 miles) inland from the Atlantic coast.

Seville's long and eventful history – particularly the days when gold flowed incessantly from Spain's New World colonies – has left it stuffed with innumerable monuments. Most conspicuous of them is the Giralda Tower, which rises out of the cathedral as a Muslim minaret below and finishes as a Christian belfry.

Down at ground level, the biggest draws are the exquisite palace of the Reales Alcázares; the quaint Barrio de Santa Cruz, a perfect cluster of narrow, shady streets through which the fragrance of orange blossom wafts delicately in spring; the legendary Maestranza Bullring; and, more viscerally, the music, dynamism and song of flamenco whose exciting, passionate presence is felt all over the city. Such are the ingredients that gave birth to the fictional characters of Carmen and Don Juan, Seville's most famous inhabitants.

It would be a mistake to see Seville as merely a city living on myths of *toreros*, libertines and gypsy flamenco dancers. Seville is – and likes to think of itself as – a thoroughly modern, hard-working city. Twice in the last hundred years (in 1929 and 1992) it has held international exhibitions to convince the world that it is up with the contemporary zeitgeist. While both have left the city with some interesting pieces of architecture, neither has made much impact on traditional Seville. This is a city that will probably leave you guessing what is real and what is cliché.

The golden horizons of the Torre del Oro

When to go

There is no wrong time to visit Seville, but bear in mind that July and August can be challenging as the (sometimes oppressive) heat drives many residents to decamp to the coast and, as a consequence, quite a few bars and cafés can close without warning. Spring is a particularly lovely time to visit because of the blossom and flowers in parks and gardens.

SEASONS & CLIMATE

This is southern Spain and you can expect it to be anything from agreeably warm to unpleasantly hot. Even in the thick of winter it rarely gets truly cold, and overcast or rainy days are the exception rather than the rule.

ANNUAL EVENTS

Southern Spain has a busy calendar of traditional fiestas. In Seville the two most important are Holy Week (see below) and, immediately after it, the April Fair (see page 12).

March & April

Semana Santa (Holy Week) Holy Week is celebrated all over Spain, but nowhere to the extent that you'll witness in Seville, where processions and street parties make for high-octane merriment.

April

La Feria de Abril (The April Fair) A flamboyant *feria* of flamenco fun that fills the city with colour and joy (see The April Fair, page 12).

⬤ *Semana Santa procession in Seville*

May & June

El Rocío On Whitsunday (some time between mid-May and mid-June, depending on the date of Easter) the little town of El Rocío (see page 108) is swamped by an army of thousands of traditionally costumed pilgrims to honour the Virgen del Rocío (Virgin of the Dew).

September

Feria de San Miguel A fair in which the city revisits some of its cultural traditions with displays of horsemanship and bullfighting

▲ *Parading the Virgin in the city's patron saint festival*

prowess at the Fundación Real Escuela Andaluza de Arte Ecuestre (Royal Horse School, see page 110).

September & October

Flamenco Biennial (every two years: 2008's is 10 Sept–11 Oct) Displays, shows and even academic conferences celebrate the joyous gypsy dance at venues throughout the city.

December

Fiesta de La Virgen de La Inmaculada (11 & 12 Dec) Choirs and teams of dancers – including, on the second day, children – pay tribute to the city's patron saint. ⓐ Pl. de Triunfo

---

PUBLIC HOLIDAYS
Año Nuevo (New Year's Day) 1 Jan
Día de Reyes (Epiphany) 6 Jan
Andalucia Day 28 Feb
Jueves Santo (Maundy Thursday) 20 Mar 2008; 9 Apr 2009
Viernes Santo (Good Friday) 21 Mar 2008; 10 Apr 2009
Día del Trabajo (Labour Day) 1 May
Virgen de los Reyes (patroness of the city; the Day of the Assumption) 15 Aug
Día de la Hispanidad (Spain's national day) 12 Oct
Todos Los Santos (All Saints' Day) 1 Nov
Día de la Constitución (Constitution Day) 6 Dec
La Inmaculada Concepción (Immaculate Conception) 8 Dec
Día de Navidad (Christmas Day) 25 Dec

The April Fair

Immediately after the excesses of Holy Week, Seville launches into an altogether different type of celebration. There's nothing religious about the April Fair. It's simply an enormous party, six intense days of hyperactivity mainly celebrating Andalucian folk culture. It's held in the fairground in the Barrio de los Remedios. Just follow the tide of people (including women in gaudy flamenco dresses) across the Puente San Telmo from Parque María Luisa or through Triana and you'll find the monumental gateway of lights.

You're welcome to wander around the streets of the fairground and savour the atmosphere, but you'll soon realise that the fair is a combination of private parties taking place in *casetas* (marquees) that are members-only, owned by societies, companies, families and other organisations. What's more, they are often patrolled by security personnel. Fortunately a few *casetas* – notably those owned by political parties – are open to the public and are essentially makeshift bars, which can easily get crowded. Most of the larger *casetas* are equipped with a dance floor. The soundtrack of the fair is the *sevillana*, a home-grown variant of flamenco.

As with all events in Spain, don't arrive too early. By mid-afternoon there is a steady stream of horse-drawn carriages rumbling around the fairground in the Paseo de Caballos and cocky *señoritos* (wearing the typical Andalucian herdsman's outfit of grey, wide-brimmed hat, tight leather breeches and a short jacket) will already be knocking back glasses of *fino* sherry, the fair's preferred tipple.

The music and the dancing get going only in the evening after the bullfight in the Plaza de Toros de la Real Maestranza (see page 81), considered an integral part of the fair. It is not just that the fairground is transformed into a spectacle of illuminations by the lanterns, or *farolillos*, along its streets, it's also that at night you are more likely to catch a glimpse of aristocrats, bullfighters, pop stars and other Spanish celebrities drawn by the glamour of the fair.

Seville's fair is undoubtedly the fair to attend, but if you can't make it or you want something less exclusive, try Jerez de la Frontera's fair, which comes shortly after and whose *casetas* are all open to the public.

On horseback at the April Fair

History

Local tradition insists that Hercules, the Greek mythological hero, founded Seville. In reality, though, it was Julius Caesar who, in 45 BC, raised what was probably a small Iberian settlement on the banks of the Guadalquivir to the status of Roman municipality. By the 4th century AD, Hispalis (as it was then known) was one of the most important cities in Spain. But as the Roman Empire crumbled, it was captured by invading hordes of barbarians: first the Vandals, then the Visigoths. Two local clergymen, saints Leander and Isidore, were instrumental in winning the latter away from the Arian heresy and over to mainstream Christianity.

When Muslim (usually known as Moorish) invaders overran Spain from North Africa in 711 they were quick to take the city, which they renamed Isbilya. In the 11th century it became capital of a kingdom that stretched from modern-day Portugal to the east coast of Spain. A fresh wave of Muslim invaders, the Almohads, made Seville their capital, and the city enjoyed another brief moment of splendour of which the famous Giralda Tower is the chief reminder.

In 1248 King Fernando III of Castile took Seville for Christianity and made it his residence. The city's mosques were converted into churches. One of his successors, Pedro I, was responsible for building the magnificent royal palace of the Reales Alcázares.

With the fall of Granada in 1492 the Reconquest of Spain was complete. That same year Columbus was dispatched on his historic voyage to the Americas. As a river port close to the Atlantic seaboard, Seville was ideally placed to profit from growing trade with the New World, and the city grew rich on the proceeds.

The good times ended in 1717 when Seville lost its monopoly to nearby Cádiz. The next centuries were hard for the economically struggling city beset by plague and floods. Its woes increased with the loss of Spain's colonies and valuable trade.

In 1929 Seville tried to rebrand itself by staging a Latin American Expo which left little behind except the Parque María Luisa and some elegant architecture. Then came the Spanish Civil War and the depressed postwar era. Seville only recovered with the advent of democracy and a new constitution; widespread devolution meant the city became the capital of Andalucia. Soon after, a local boy, Felipe Gonzalez, became prime minister of Spain.

Since the heady summer of Expo 92 (see below), Seville has been feeling its way in the world, attempting to cling on to its traditions while giving itself a thoroughly modern makeover. Indeed, in October 2006, the city's mayor, Alfredo Sánchez Monteseirín, unveiled a massive modernisation scheme for Seville.

EXPO 92

Expo 92, held from spring to autumn 1992, was visited by around 41 million people. The nominated site on the Isla de la Cartuja was landscaped and transformed by pavilions built by some of the 111 nations participating as well as other supposedly futuristic buildings, some of which have since been put to other uses. Other visible signs of the passing of the Expo are Santa Justa railway station and the high-speed AVE (Alta Velocidad Española) rail link with Madrid, an expanded airport and six striking bridges across the river. However, Expo 92 has proved a hard act to live up to and, more than 15 years since its final whistle, the debate about its ultimate worth to the city still rages.

Lifestyle

Sevillanos like to think they are hard-working, but they are also proud of their capacity for going at their own pace and enjoying themselves. The climate imposes a certain rhythm to life and you'll be wise to go with it – particularly in summer when the heat makes it difficult to do anything in a hurry.

A Seville day begins slowly and the morning is long. Lunchtime is late compared with most other countries. Only touristy restaurants start serving before 14.00 and it is not unusual to sit down to a full meal after 15.00.

A long digestive break follows with or without a siesta according to personal preference and the weather. In the summer it makes sense to take a nap in the heat of the day so as to be refreshed and ready to go out when the temperature becomes bearable again in the evening.

The afternoon begins at 16.00–17.00 and many people still have half a working day ahead of them before clocking off at around 21.00.

Dinner is around 22.00–23.00, but is not as heavy as lunch. If the gap between meals becomes interminable, you can always fill it with a few tapas.

To keep up with the locals it's best to adjust to their rhythm and do as they do. Don't try to do everything in one day, give yourself occasional time off, and be prepared for a late night if you want to see the city at its most relaxed.

Although some of the locals can seem brusque at times this is often because they are slightly fazed by dealing with so many tourists who don't speak their language. Most people you meet will be only too helpful. Keep a smile on your face, adopt the local manners and don't be too quick to take offence and you'll get what you want. Particularly important in this gregarious country is to show respect for other people. Always say 'hello' when you enter a shop, bar or any other public place: *buenos días* during the day and *buenas tardes* (good afternoon/evening) from 19.00–20.00 onwards. And don't forget to say *adiós* when you leave.

△ *Enjoy a leisurely lunch on the terrace of El Faro de Triana (see page 100)*

Culture

Although Seville is a modern city with a contemporary culture, it takes most of its inspiration from the past and from its tradition. In particular, its greatest creative age was the 17th century, the period of baroque when New World riches paid for artworks to furnish palaces, churches and monasteries. One of Spain's greatest painters, Velázquez, was born in Seville although he spent the greater part of his life around the court in Madrid. Much more intimately associated with the city of their birth are the painters Francisco de Zurbarán (1598–1662), Bartolomé Murillo (1617–82) and Juan de Valdés Leal (1662–95), and the sculptor Juan Martínez Montañez (1568–1648). Invariably, given the times in which they lived, these artists were commissioned to portray religious themes but there is great variety in their approaches. While Murillo, for instance, often verges on sentimentality, Zurbarán is widely thought to have brought a sense of spirituality to his work and Valdés Leal's paintings are strikingly expressive and dramatic, executed with a decisive hand and exploiting strong contrasts in colour and shade.

Seville has two other cultural streams of influence that were once looked down on but have recently acquired respectability. One of these is the music and dance of flamenco, which originated as a marginal gypsy form of song and dance but which has now been assimilated into the mainstream and exported all over the world.

The other cultural revival concerns Seville's Muslim (and to some extent Jewish) past. The Christian Reconquest of Spain at the end of the 15th century was meant to be the definitive end of the Moors and their civilisation, and thereafter few people were interested in

▶ *Don Juan, Seville's most famous (or infamous) literary son*

anything not born out of Catholic Christianity. But since the death of Franco (a devout Catholic) and the restoration of democracy, Seville has been busy unearthing and putting on display various treasures from its former Muslim self. From time to time there are exhibitions on Al Andalus (Muslim Spain) in venues in Seville, but there are also some permanent reminders that the Christians weren't the only ones to leave us with evidence of an acute artistic sensibility. Several churches have strongly suggestive traces – not to mention emphatic statements – in their architecture and ornamentation of the mosques that they once were.

DON JUAN

The fictional character of archetypal, heart-stealing lecher, Don Juan, 'the Trickster of Seville', was dreamt up by priest and playwright Tirso de Molina in the early 17th century. His creation soon acquired a life of his own. Indeed, he stars in subsequent works by Molière, Mozart and George Bernard Shaw among others, and appears in books, films and even a ballet. More than just an unchecked Latin lover, Don Juan is a complex person who has been described as very un-Spanish in the way he destructively pursues his own goals without regard to the norms of society. 'He is hardly a character at all – but a universal day-dream or myth,' wrote VS Pritchett, who went on to reveal perhaps more about himself than Don Juan by adding: 'He expresses the male desire for inexhaustible sexual vitality, the female desire to be ravished against the will, reason, interest or honour.'

▶ *The inner courtyard of the Palacio de la Condesa de Lebrija*

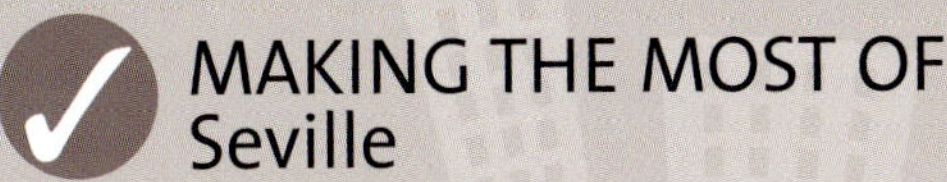

MAKING THE MOST OF
Seville

Shopping

The city's main shopping area centres on two more or less parallel streets, Sierpes and Tetuán/Velázquez, which run from the town hall on Plaza San Francisco and Plaza Nueva north to the squares of La Campana and Duque de la Victoria. The shops also spread down neighbouring streets towards Plaza de Alfalfa and, in the opposite direction, towards the river. Here you'll find just about everything you'll need: men's and women's fashions, shoes, ceramics and other crafts, jewellery and assorted souvenirs. Seville city centre still has many fascinating smaller, and specialised, shops that haven't yet been driven out by national and international brand-name chain stores.

If you don't know where else to look, try El Corte Inglés department store on Plaza del Duque de la Victoria (see page 69) or one of the big three shopping centres: Plaza de Armas (closest to the centre, see page 87), Nervión Plaza (see page 87) or **Los Arcos** (Ⓦ www.cclosarcos.com) (further out, continuing past Nervión Plaza).

By far the best street market is El Jueves, which is held, as its name says, on Thursdays in the Calle Feria in the Barrio de La Macarena.

⬤ *A hand-painted fan is a wonderful souvenir*

Principally, it's an antiques market but there are many smaller collectable items for sale and, if nothing else, it's worth attending for the atmosphere.

Craft goods associated with Seville include ceramics (see page 97), *mantones* (shawls, for going out at night or attending the April Fair, see page 12), lace *mantillas* (traditionally worn during Holy Week and by bridesmaids), *bordados* (embroidery), *encajes* (lacework), fans (often hand-painted), guitars, and flamenco dresses and accessories. Other possible items to take home are bullfighting posters, religious statues, olive oil, wine, sherry and cured Spanish hams.

USEFUL SHOPPING PHRASES

What time do the shops open/close?
¿A qué hora abren/cierran las tiendas?
¿A kay ora abren/theeyerran las teeyendas?

How much is this?
¿Cuánto vale?
¿Cwantoe baleh?

Can I try this on?
¿Puedo probarme esto?
¿Pwedo probarme esto?

My size is ...
Mi número es el ...
Mee noomairo es el ...

I'll take this one, thank you
Me llevo éste, gracias
Meh llievo esteh, gratheeas

This is too large/too small/too expensive. Do you have any others?
Es muy grande/muy pequeño/muy caro. ¿Tienen otros?
Es mooy grandeh/mooy pekenio/mooy karo. ¿Teeyenen ohtross?

Eating & drinking

Installing yourself in a succession of bars, cafés and restaurants is one of the delights of a visit to Seville. The city has a wide choice of places to eat and drink – from the old-fashioned and quaint, to the vibrantly modern.

The city takes pride in its number and variety of bars and restaurants catering for all tastes and budgets. They go by several different names – including *asador* (indicating that meat is roasted

● *Locals enjoy a drink in El Rinconcillo (see page 88)*

> **PRICE CATEGORIES**
> The price guides given whenever a restaurant is mentioned
> indicate the approximate price of a three-course meal (*menú
> del día* if there is one) for one person, excluding drinks, but
> including tax.
> £ up to €20   ££ €20–40   £££ over €40

in a wood-fired oven), *mesón* (an antiquated word for an inn), *cervezería* (specialising in beers) and *bodega* or *bodeguita* (specialising in wines).

For the most part, the cuisine is 'typically Andalucian' – which means straightforward meat, fish, seafood and vegetable dishes prepared and served with the minimum of complication and formality. With such an abundance of good fresh ingredients to hand there's no need to disguise them with rich sauces. As this is southern Spain most dishes have olive oil lurking in them somewhere and dairy foods are used minimally.

If you don't like the local food or want a change from it, the city has a good choice of restaurants specialising in the cuisines of other parts of Spain and an array of international restaurants including Chinese, Japanese, Latin American, Italian and, inevitably, fast food.

The main meal in Spain is eaten in the middle of the day. This is when most restaurants offer a cheaper menu, *menú del día*, which typically consists of three courses with a bottle of the house wine included. This is certainly the best way to fill up without spending a lot of money. Note that a *menú de degustación* is something altogether different. Only seen in high-class restaurants, it is a pricey sampler menu.

Where Seville excels is in its tapas bars, the fast-food joints of Spain. Even posh restaurants are likely to have a bar attached where you can eat well without having to order a full meal. Order what you want – if you want a larger portion ask for a *ración* of it – and pay for what you have eaten and drunk at the end. But take care: tapas can easily add up to more than the cost of a *menú del día*. The big thing about tapas is that they are available any time of day or night. You'll never hear anyone in Seville tell you the kitchen is closed and there's nothing to eat!

Tapas are often a godsend to vegetarians visiting Spain. If nothing else, almost every bar can provide a *ración* of meat-free salad or a slice of the old stand-by, *tortilla de patata* (potato omelette).

To go with the tapas, Spain has an increasingly good choice of wines, many of them economically priced. Imported bottles, by contrast, are rarely seen and are expensive. If there is a Sevillian drink par excellence, it has to be *fino* sherry – a dry fortified wine made in Jerez and drunk chilled.

Spain's main gastronomic failing is its dessert menu, which all too often reduces to a piece of fresh fruit, a scoop of ice cream or the ubiquitous flan – crème caramel. But it makes up for this deficiency by being strong on sweet snacks. Seville has several excellent cake shops, *pastelerías*, offering a choice of something to go with a coffee or to fill the long gap between lunch and dinner. The best known of them is La Campana (see page 72).

Another weak point for many visitors – particularly British – is breakfast. Many Spaniards eat hardly anything when they first get up, preferring instead to have a sandwich or snack mid-morning. A few bars do open early and serve a reasonably good breakfast of toast, coffee and fresh orange juice. A popular alternative to this is a portion of *churros* – deep fried sticks of batter that are sprinkled with sugar and dunked into a cup of coffee or hot chocolate.

USEFUL DINING PHRASES

I would like a table for ... people
Quisiera una mesa para ... personas
Keyseeyera oona mesa para ... personas

May I have the bill, please?
¿Podría traerme la cuenta
por favor?
*¿Podreea tryairme la cwenta
por fabor?*

Waiter/waitress!
¡Camarero/Camarera!
¡Camareroe/Camarera!

Could I have it well-cooked/medium/rare please?
¿Por favor, la carne bien hecha/al punto/poco hecha?
¿Por fabor, la kahrneh beeyen etcha/al poontoh/poko etcha?

I am a vegetarian. Does this contain meat?
Soy vegetariano. ¿Tiene carne este plato?
Soy behetahreeahnoh. ¿Teeyeneh carneh esteh plahtoh?

Where is the toilet (restroom) please?
¿Dónde están los servicios, por favor?
¿Dondeh estan los serbeetheeos, por fabor?

I would like a cup of/two cups of/another coffee/tea
Quisiera una taza de/dos tazas de/otra taza de café/té
*Keyseeyera oona tatha dey/dos tathas dey/otra tatha
dey kafey/tey*

Entertainment & nightlife

Largely due to the climate, but also because of the pattern of the working day, nights out begin late in Seville and go on later – especially in summer when daytime temperatures are too hot to do anything except cower indoors.

At any time of year the street life may be enough to entertain you, but there are always regular live-performance venues to draw you in complemented by a busy programme of special events. Everything is listed or advertised in various publications available

⬇ *Ceramic sign for one of the city's flamenco bars*

free from tourist information offices. The best and most complete of them is *El Giradillo* (ⓦ www.elgiradillo.es), which is almost entirely in Spanish but still intelligible to a non-speaker.

The largest entertainment venue in the city is **El Auditorio** (ⓣ (954) 46 74 08 ⓦ www.auditoriodesevilla.com) in the Isla de la Cartuja theatre, which stages a diversity of events including most types of music.

The city's three main theatres (all of which sometimes have concerts to complement their programmes of plays) are, in order of artistic significance:

Teatro Central (ⓐ C/ José de Gálvez 6, Isla de la Cartuja ⓣ (954) 46 08 80 ⓦ www.teatrocentral.com), **Teatro Lope de Vega** (ⓐ Av. María Luisa ⓣ (954) 59 08 53 ⓦ www.teatrolopedevega.org) and **Teatro de la Maestranza** (ⓐ Paseo Colón 22 ⓣ (954) 22 65 73 ⓦ www.teatromaestranza.com).

Perhaps more interesting is the small, innovative, independent theatre **Sala La Imperdible** (ⓐ Pl. San Antonio de Padua 9 ⓣ (954) 38 82 19 ⓦ www.imperdible.org).

The two golden rules for enjoying the nightlife of Seville are not to go out too early – certainly not before 23.00 – and not to drink too much. Many people like to start the evening in one or more *bares de copas*. These are bars for drinking (shorts rather than beers and wines) which don't generally serve tapas. They can be distinguished from everyday bars not only by their late opening hours but also because they have few chairs, not too much light, preened bar staff and loud music on the speakers, possibly controlled by a DJ. Only after midnight or later do people move on to the clubs – although be sure to call them *discotecas* because 'club' in Spanish sometimes has connotations of a roadside brothel.

Seville's James Bonds gather at the **Gran Casino Aljarafe**
(ⓐ Av. de la Arboleda in Tomares, just outside the city ❶ (902) 42 42 22
ⓦ www.grancasinoaljarafe.com). Further away, by the seaside at
Puerto de Santa María near Cádiz is the **Casino Bahía de Cádiz**
(❶ (956) 87 10 42 ⓦ www.casinobahiadecadiz.es).

If you fancy taking in a movie, most films screened in cinemas
and on television are dubbed into Spanish, but you can often see
original version ('VO') English-language films (with Spanish subtitles)
at **Avenida 5 Cines** (ⓐ C/ Marqués de Paradas 15 ❶ (954) 29 30 25).

FLAMENCO

Flamenco is the music, song and dance of Andalucia, particularly
of the gypsy community. It is associated especially with the
provinces of Seville and Cádiz. The rough wailing voice of the
singer is often unaccompanied except by rhythmic clapping,
but to this is often added the rapid strumming of a guitar.
Songs are never less than full-on passionate and express a
range of emotions, mainly sadness and torment. Sometimes
the singer and guitarist provide the soundtrack for a dancer –
usually female. In true flamenco style, neither the song nor
the dance follows a prescribed script. They are never done
exactly the same way twice and performers continue for
as long as their emotions dictate and stamina allows.

The flamenco shows in Santa Cruz are for tourists but
nonetheless good. In Triana it can be more authentic. In Calle
Salado you can dance *sevillanas* – pacy folk dances. Purists
would say you have to be in the right place at the right time
for a spontaneous performance of the real thing.

Sport & relaxation

With its benign climate and abundance of green space, Seville is perfect for watching or taking part in outdoor activities. Its various parks are good places to stroll, run, cycle or rollerblade. Try the green strip beside the river starting near the Puente de Isabel II and continuing beyond the Plaza de Armas shopping centre (see page 87), and the extensive **Parque del Alamillo** (ⓦ www.parquedelalamillo.org) at the northern end of the Isla de Cartuja.

SPECTATOR SPORTS

Football

The city has two rival teams: FC Sevilla (which plays at the **Estadio Ramón Sanchez-Pizjuán** ⓐ Luis de Morales ⓣ (902) 50 19 01 ⓦ www.sevillafc.es) and Real Betis (which plays at the **Estadio Manuel Ruíz de Lopera** in Heliopolis, south of the city centre ⓣ (954) 61 03 40 ⓦ www.realbetisbalompie.es).

Bullfighting

Newcomers to Spain often don't know what to make of bullfighting, but then many Spaniards don't either. On TV and in the newspapers it's treated as a form of art combining the noblest elements of a spectator sport. Attending a bullfight is respectable almost to the point of being chic. On the other hand, it is easy to condemn *la corrida* as ritualised animal cruelty of the most cynical kind. Perhaps the only thing to do is see a bullfight for yourself and make up your own mind. As Seville has the most famous bullring in the country (see page 81), there is no better place to see what the fuss is about. The season runs from Easter to October with an important series of bullfights during the April Fair (see page 12).

⬤ *Make up your own mind about Spain's traditional national sport*

PARTICIPATION SPORTS

Golf

The 72-par course of the **Real Club de Golf de Sevilla** (ⓐ Autovía Sevilla-
Utrera, Alcalá de Guadaira ⓣ (954) 12 43 01 ⓦ www.sevillagolf.com)
is ranked as the third-best golf course in Spain and has hosted the
WGC World Cup.

RELAXATION

Turkish baths

If you need to unwind, Seville has two Turkish baths. The most
conveniently located is **Aire de Sevilla** (ⓐ Aire 15 ⓣ (955) 01 00 25
ⓦ www.airedesevilla.com), which is on an extremely narrow street
in the middle of Santa Cruz and has a tea room (see page 71).
Medina Aljarafe (ⓐ Hernán Cortés 12, Bormujos ⓣ (954) 78 83 44
ⓣ www.medinaaljarafe.com) is on the outskirts of the city.

Accommodation

Seville offers a good choice of places to stay in all price ranges, which is unusual for large Spanish cities.

Hotels are officially ranked from 1 to 5 stars, but this doesn't tell you much except the quantity of facilities. Atmosphere and the standard of service do not always correspond to stars, and neither do prices. Seville's hotels – including almost all its boutique hotels in converted old houses – are concentrated in the picturesque and touristy Santa Cruz quarter (see page 60). This means that all the sights – and the best bars and restaurants – are within easy walking distance.

Generally cheaper are *hostales* (not to be confused with youth hostels), also known as *pensiones*. These are guesthouses that usually have en suite rooms but are unlikely to have 24-hour reception or room service and may not offer any meals apart from breakfast.

A well-kept family-run *pensión* or *hostal* can be a friendlier place to stay and often represents good value for money.

HOTELS

Arias £ If you want to be in the city centre and don't mind forgoing a few luxuries in favour of a good price, this may be the place to be. ⓐ Mariana de Pineda 9 ⓣ (954) 22 68 40 ⓦ www.hostalarias.com

PRICE CATEGORIES

The price symbols indicate the approximate price of an en suite room for two people for one night in high season, including tax.

£ up to €60   ££ €60–120   £££ over €120

Casa Sol y Luna £ Unusually for Seville, the Sol y Luna is a great-value *pensión*, with characterful rooms (though not all are en suite) in a converted mansion. ⓐ Pérez Galdós 1A ⓣ (954) 21 06 82 ⓦ www.casasolyluna1.com

Sierpes £ A *hostal* in Santa Cruz that represents a good compromise between price and comforts. The en suite rooms surround a typical Andalucian patio. There is a café and restaurant and, usefully for central Seville, a garage. ⓐ Corral del Rey 22 ⓣ (954) 22 49 48 ⓦ www.hsierpes.com

Alcántara ££ A modernised 18th-century mansion with 21 guestrooms in the middle of Santa Cruz. ⓐ Ximénez de Enciso 28 ⓣ (954) 50 05 95 ⓦ www.hotelalcantara.net

Amadeus ££ A hotel by and for music lovers occupying an 18th-century house near Iglesia Santa Cruz. Each of the individually decorated 14 rooms is named after a composer and concerts are held regularly. Upstairs there is a terrace with views. ⓐ Farnesio 6 ⓣ (954) 50 14 43 ⓦ www.hotelamadeussevilla.com

La Casa del Maestro ££ This city centre house was supposedly built in 1890 by a nobleman for one of his illegitimate children and was later owned by flamenco guitarist Niño Ricardo. All rooms have high ceilings; some have four-poster beds. ⓐ Almudena 5 ⓣ (954) 50 00 07 ⓦ www.lacasadelmaestro.com

Goya ££ A clean, functional air-conditioned *hostal* in Santa Cruz with 19 rooms equipped with television and phone. ⓐ Mateos Gago 31 ⓣ (954) 21 11 70 ⓦ www.hostalgoyasevilla.com

⬤ *The Hostería del Laurel is in the heart of the Santa Cruz district*

Hostería del Laurel ££ A 22-room hotel and restaurant (see page 74) in one of the picturesque squares at the heart of Santa Cruz. ⓐ Pl. de los Venerables 5 ⓣ (954) 22 02 95 ⓦ www.hosteriadellaurel.com

Hotel Alminar ££ A tiny, very friendly hotel close to La Giralda. Rooms are simply but comfortably decorated, and excellent value for the price. ⓐ Álvarez Quintero 52 ⓣ (954) 29 39 13 ⓦ www.hotelalminar.com

Murillo ££ Named after one of Seville's most famous painters and furnished in an old-fashioned style with armour and antiques, the

Murillo has 14 one- or two-bedroom apartments equipped for self-catering. In the Santa Cruz quarter. ⓐ Lope de Rueda 9 ⓣ (954) 21 60 95 ⓦ www.hotelmurillo.com

Sacristía Santa Ana ££ Seville's newest boutique hotel, where the reasonable prices belie the attention to detail and spaciousness of the rooms, around a galleried courtyard. Located in the city centre. ⓐ Alameda de Hércules 22 ⓣ (954) 91 57 22 ⓦ www.sacristiadesantaana.com

Simón ££ An elegant but not overly formal old house in the centre of the city, just west of the cathedral. Suites with sitting rooms and quadruple rooms available. Good value. ⓐ García de Vinuesa 19 ⓣ (954) 22 66 60 ⓦ www.hotelsimonsevilla.com

Petit Palace Santa Cruz ££–£££ The Petit Palace chain prides itself on being high-tech, and every room has free internet access. Décor verges on the masculine, but rooms are centred around a porticoed patio in typically *sevillano* style. ⓐ Muñoz y Pabón 18 ⓣ (954) 22 10 32 ⓦ www.hthoteles.com

Alcoba del Rey de Sevilla £££ Neo-oriental boutique hotel near the Macarena basilica. The 15 rooms are all different and the bathrooms are worthy of note. And if you like anything you see in the hotel – even the beds, taps or floors – you can buy it and take it home with you. ⓐ Bécquer 9 ⓣ (954) 91 58 00 ⓦ www.alcobadelrey.com

Casa Imperial £££ A converted 16th-century mansion adjacent to the Casa de Pilatos in the city centre consisting of 24 individually decorated suites, some with a private terrace. ⓐ Imperial 29 ⓣ (954) 50 03 00 ⓦ www.casaimperial.com

▲ *Top-class accommodation at the Hotel Alfonso XIII*

Las Casas del Rey de Baeza £££ An 18th-century mansion on a cobbled square in the centre, with a classical façade and a peaceful courtyard. Spacious bedrooms, good breakfast and bonus: a small, open-air pool on the roof. ⓐ Pl. Jesús de la Redención 2 ⓣ (954) 56 14 96 ⓦ www.hospes.es

Convento La Gloria £££ Once a 15th-century convent, this is now a pretty boutique hotel, with many of the original features. It's a stone's throw from La Giralda, which some of its 35 rooms overlook. ⓐ Argote de Molina ⓣ (954) 29 36 70 ⓦ www.hotelconventolagloria.com

Doña María £££ Nowhere else in Seville can you swim or have drinks and tapas by the poolside while enjoying a view of the cathedral and

Giralda. Each room is dedicated to a famous woman from Seville's history. ⓐ Don Remondo 19 ⓣ (954) 22 49 90 ⓦ www.hdmaria.com

Hotel Alfonso XIII £££ The classic luxury hotel of Seville with all the comforts its VIP guests could ask for, including a poolside bar and two restaurants – one of them Japanese (see page 78). ⓐ San Fernando 2 ⓣ (954) 91 70 00 ⓦ www.hotel-alfonsoxiii.com

Posada del Lucero £££ A 16th-century city-centre inn newly converted into a bitingly modern hotel, its rooms decorated in shades of taupe and mahogany, with black slate in the bathrooms and walnut furniture. ⓐ Almirante Apodaca 7 ⓣ (954) 502 480 ⓦ www.posadadellucero.com

Taberna del Alabardero £££ This hotel northwest of the cathedral occupies the sensitively restored 19th-century house of a renowned Seville poet. It has seven comfortable rooms, each one of which is named after a different province of Andalucia. ⓐ Zaragoza 20 ⓣ (954) 50 27 21 ⓦ www.tabernadelalabardero.com

YOUTH HOSTELS

Oasis Backpackers Hostel £ Claims always to have space for walk-in guests. Breakfast is included in the price. Located in the city centre. ⓐ C/ Alonso el Sabio 1A ⓣ (954) 29 37 77 ⓦ www.oasissevilla.com

CAMPSITES

The closest campsites to Seville are:

Camping Club de Campo ⓐ en Av. de la Libertad, Carretera Sevilla-Cádiz, Dos Hermanas ⓣ (954) 72 02 50

Camping Oromana ⓐ Camino del Maestre, Alcalá de Guadaira ⓣ (955) 68 32 57 ⓦ www.campingoromana.com

THE BEST OF SEVILLE

Whether you are on a flying visit to Seville or taking a more leisurely break in southern Spain, here are some of the sights and activities you should try not to miss.

TOP 10 ATTRACTIONS

- **Barrio de Santa Cruz** A picture-postcard-pretty complex of streets and squares (see page 60)

- **Cathedral y Giralda (Cathedral and the Giralda)** Two sights in one. The Giralda is essentially a topped-up minaret with a ramp leading all the way to the top. The tower makes a handy landmark to get your bearings. The massive Gothic cathedral below contains the tomb of (parts of) Christopher Columbus (see page 63)

- **Spring fiestas** Two very different celebrations fall close together, both of them spectacular. First come the processions of Holy Week (see page 8). Shortly afterwards comes the exuberant April Fair (see page 12)

- **Flamenco** The emblematic music and dance of southern Spain comes in many forms but is always performed with passion. There are plenty of places where you can see a show. And there is a museum to explain it (see page 68)

- **Museo de Bellas Artes (Museum of Fine Arts)** One of the great art galleries of Spain, concentrating on Seville's 'Golden Age' painters (see page 84)

- **Plaza de España** An extravagantly tiled monument in celebration of Spain in all its facets, this is the most prominent building in the leafy Parque de María Luisa, former showground of an international exhibition (see page 79)

- **Plaza de Toros de la Real Maestranza** The most famous bullring in the world. It's best to see it when packed out for a top *corrida*, but you can take a guided tour of it at any time (see page 81)

- **Reales Alcázares** An exquisite royal palace built by the Christian kings of Castile in glorious Moorish style. The oldest occupied royal palace in Europe. It also has beautiful gardens (see page 66)

- **Río Guadalquivir** Seville wouldn't be Seville without its river, which is crossed by nine bridges. You can take a trip down it, stroll along its banks, or sit on a terrace of a bar or restaurant and take in a view of it at your leisure (see page 92)

- **Torre del Oro** There's not much to the short little 'Golden Tower' on the riverbank, but it's still a Seville landmark (see page 82)

Suggested itineraries

HALF-DAY: SEVILLE IN A HURRY

If you have only a morning or afternoon in Seville, there's no choice to make. Spend it in the Barrio de Santa Cruz (see page 60), but go up the Giralda Tower (see page 63) as well. If you're quick, you may be able to get around the Reales Alcázares (see page 66), next door to the cathedral, as well. Santa Cruz has innumerable tapas bars and restaurants where you can grab a bite to eat to begin or end your visit.

1 DAY: TIME TO SEE A LITTLE MORE

With a whole day in Seville your best option is to stay in Santa Cruz and see the half-day itinerary at your leisure. You should also be able to stroll down to the riverside and see the Torre del Oro and bullring (see pages 82 and 81).

2–3 DAYS: TIME TO SEE MUCH MORE

One day will be spent as above, but the extra days will give you a chance to do more. Depending on your interest, you may choose to visit Triana, the Museo de Bellas Artes (see page 84) or the Parque de María Luisa (see page 79). You could also take a day trip out of the city, perhaps to see Doñana National Park (see page 108) or even Córdoba.

LONGER: ENJOYING SEVILLE TO THE FULL

With a week or more you'll have time to fit in everything you want to see and do. If this is your first visit to southern Spain, try to get over to Granada for a day or two. You may want to spend another couple of days exploring Ronda and the white towns.

NO8DO

Almost everywhere you go in Seville you'll see a symbol like some slick, inscrutable brand name carved on walls and written on posters: NO8DO.

Rather than a modern commercial invention it is a civic insignia that has been in use since the 13th century. Traditionally – and no one has yet come up with a better theory – it is held to be a mark of gratitude from King Alfonso X the Wise to the city for staying loyal to him during a struggle for the succession. It almost needs a competent texter to interpret it. The '8' stands for a skein of wool or *madeja* and so the message reads: *No-madeja-do* or *no me ha dejado* – that is, 'She [Seville] hasn't abandoned me.'

△ *How many of these can you spot around the city?*

Something for nothing

To see the best of Seville you don't have to spend money. You can enjoy its charm simply by strolling around its streets, squares and gardens. The Santa Cruz quarter is the obvious place to spend most time, but window shopping in the city centre also has its interest. If you've got time on your hands but no cash in your pockets, other good places to walk and see sights for free are the riverbanks and bridges of the Guadalquivir, Parque de María Luisa (especially the Plaza de España) and the former Expo 92 grounds on the Isla de Cartuja, which have a sort of postmodern fascination.

Plan ahead and you can see many of the city's essential monuments and museums without parting with a penny. Some of those that are not free all the time have a particular day of the week on which they waive the admission charge. The Archivo General de Indias (see page 68), Basílica de la Macarena (see page 76) and Hotel Alfonso XIII (see page 78) are free all the time to everyone. The Museo de Bellas Artes (see page 84) and the Archaeological Museum (see page 84) are free to citizens of EU countries. The Centro Andaluz de Arte Contemporáneo (see page 98) on the Isla de Cartuja is free to EU citizens on Tuesdays (its grounds are free at any time), and the Torre del Oro (see page 82) and the Casa de Pilatos (Tuesday afternoons only, see page 62) are also free that day. The cathedral (see page 63) is free on Sundays.

If you do your research well, you can turn the situation to your advantage and go in search of sights that other visitors might not bother with. La Macarena has several old churches, for instance, with vestiges of the mosques over which they were built. The Plaza de Armas shopping centre (see page 87) is the handsome old engine shed of a former railway station. Even in the middle of much transited Santa Cruz are three neglected Roman columns, immensely tall and rising out of a lush green pit in the ground on Calle Mármoles.

If you happen to be in Seville in spring, you will have all the street entertainment you want for free: first the semi-solemn semi-jubilant processions of Holy Week (see page 8); then the troops of gaudily dressed women heading on foot and in horse-drawn carriages for the showground of the April Fair (see page 12).

⬆ *Enjoy a stroll in the Parque de María Luisa*

When it rains

In summer, you'll probably be grateful for a little rain to cool things down. But at any other time of year, a few wet days can dampen your expectations of seeing a city in which sunshine and blue skies are the norm. Seville just isn't the same under brooding skies and it is as well to have a back-up plan to turn a disadvantage into a positive.

The obvious thing to do is take refuge in a museum such as the Museo de Bellas Artes (see page 84), Flamenco Museum (see page 68), Archaeological Museum (see page 84) or Palacio de la Condesa de Lebrija (see page 68). Similarly, the Archivo General de Indias (see page 68) and cathedral (see page 63) are also places you can get the best out of whatever the weather is doing. The Casa de Pilatos (see page 62), Reales Alcázares (see page 66) and Centro Andaluz de Arte Contemporáneo (see page 98) offer at least something on a rainy day, although you won't see their outdoor spaces at their best.

Alternatively, you could forget sightseeing altogether and get down to some serious shopping. If you don't want to get wet hopping between shops it may be best to confine yourself to a department store such as El Corte Inglés (see page 69) or a shopping centre where you can keep dry as long as your money holds out. All have a good choice of bars and restaurants in which you can prolong your visit. The Plaza de Armas (see page 87) is the city's most convenient and pleasant shopping centre, but you may want somewhere larger – in which case head for Nervión Plaza (see page 87) which has a cinema next to it, or, further still, past Nervión Plaza, Los Arcos (see page 22).

Another option is to find yourself a pleasant bar (not hard to do in Seville) and either strike up a conversation with the locals or sit out the showers with a good book.

If you prefer to indulge yourself with physical pleasure while it pours down outside you can retreat into one of the city's Turkish baths (see page 33).

On a rainy evening when you feel like going out, try one of the flamenco shows in Santa Cruz or El Arenal.

The Archivo General de Indias is a good bet if you're unlucky enough to get rain

On arrival

Most visitors to Seville arrive at either the airport (a bus or taxi ride from the centre) or the railway station (just within walking distance). Either way, unless you already have a hotel to go to, the best thing to do is to make for the cathedral marked by the distinctive Giralda Tower and find your bearings there.

TIME DIFFERENCE

Like the rest of Spain, Seville follows Central European Time (CET), which is one hour ahead of Greenwich Mean Time (GMT+1).

ARRIVING

By air

National and international flights arrive at **San Pablo Airport**, 5 km (3 miles) east of the city on the road to Córdoba and Madrid (❶ (954) 44 90 00 Ⓦ www.aena.es).

The quickest way to get into the city, depending on the traffic, is to take a taxi from an official rank. Buses between the city centre and the airport are run by **Los Amarillos** (❶ (902) 21 03 17) and run from approximately 06.15 to 11.00.

By rail

Seville's principal railway station is **Santa Justa** on Avenida de Kansas City (❶ (902) 24 02 02), about 20 minutes' walk east of the city centre (or a short bus ride). High-speed AVE trains from Madrid arrive here (❶ (954) 54 03 03) as well as trains from cities closer by including Jerez, Cádiz and Córdoba. There is another much smaller railway station, San Bernardo, in front of the Hospital Virgen del Rocío. Spain's main rail operator is **RENFE** (❶ (902) 24 02 02).

🔺 *Seville's main railway station, Santa Justa*

By road

If you arrive by coach you will be dropped off at one of the city's
two bus stations:

Plaza de Armas ⓐ Cristo de la Expiración ⓣ (954) 90 77 37 or
(954) 90 80 40 (services mainly from western Spain and Madrid)

El Prado de San Sebastián ⓐ Manuel Vázquez Sagastizábal
ⓣ (954) 41 71 11 or 18 (from other destinations)

If you have to drive into Seville, it's best to have a secure parking
place lined up and head straight for it. Avoid rush hour and driving
in the twisting streets of Santa Cruz and La Macarena. If there is

a quieter time to be driving in the city it is during the lunch break, around 15.00–16.00.

FINDING YOUR FEET

Seville is a lively, busy city and inevitably, like any big city, it has its criminals on the lookout for easy prey. That said, you should have no problems if you always keep your bag and camera close to you and don't stop in a dark alley to look at your map.

ORIENTATION

It's worth spending your first hour or so in the city becoming familiar with the layout, especially before you plunge into the labyrinthine streets of Santa Cruz. The cathedral and its Giralda Tower are always the main point of reference, and the river means you can never stray too far to the west. ❶ Note that many maps of Seville show the river running horizontally across them with east at the top, not north.

GETTING AROUND

In most cases the best way to get from sight to sight is to walk. Certainly, in Santa Cruz you have no other option to the further points of the Parque de María Luisa (see page 79) and to the Isla de la Cartuja (see page 92). But one of the great pleasures of Seville is to wander without haste, discovering little-known bars and shops on your way. The city is full of details – particularly ceramic murals – that not even some of the locals notice. When you want to rest your feet, you can choose from buses, taxis, bikes and boats. A previous attempt to construct a metro system was abandoned in the 1970s because of fears of damage to historic buildings. In 1999, a new project was started but progress is painfully slow.

IF YOU GET LOST, TRY ...

Excuse me, do you speak English?
Perdone, ¿habla usted inglés?
Perdoneh, ¿ahbla oosted eengless?

Excuse me, is this the right way to the Old Town/the city centre/the tourist office/the station/the bus station?
Perdone, ¿por aquí se va al casco antiguo/al centro de la ciudad/a la oficina de turísmo/a la estación de trenes/a la estación de autobuses?
Perdoneh, ¿por akee seh ba al kasko anteegwo/al thentroe dey la theeoodad/a la offeetheena dey toorismoe/a la estatheeon dey treness/a la estatheeon dey owtoebooses?

Can you point to it on my map?
¿Puede señalármelo en el mapa?
¿Pwaydeh senyalarmayloe en el mapa?

Bus services are efficient except when the traffic snarls up during rush hours or because of work on Seville's forthcoming light railway and tram system. You can pay the driver for each journey on boarding or buy a card valid for ten journeys from *estancos* (tobacconists, marked *Tabac*). There are also three- and seven-day passes available. The most useful route is C4, which circles round the city centre. There is a concentration of bus stops around the Puerta de Jerez at the end of Avenida Constitución (for info ☎ (900) 85 55 58 ⓦ www.consorciotransportes-sevilla.com).

Seville
0   100 metres
0   100 yards
Jardines del Guadalquivir
Convento de San Clemente
Auditorio
Monasterio de Santa Maria de las Cuevas
Meandro de San Jerónimo
Convento de Santa Clara
CALLE DEL TORNEO
CALLE DE SANTA CLARA
CALLE LUMBRERAS
CALLE CALATRAVA
CALLE DEL PERAL
CALLE DE LA FERIA
CALLE TORRES
CALLE PARRAS
CALLE DE RELATOR
C ANTONIO SUSILLO
CALLE MENDIG
CALLE DEL GUADALQUIVIR
CALLE DE SAN VICENTE
CALLE TEODOSIO
C MATA
C DE STA RUFINA
C DE LA FERIA
AMARGURA
CALLE ARRAYAN
C Reparad
CALLE DE SANTA ANA
C DE LAS BECAS
C DEL HOMBRE DE PIEDRA
ALAMEDA DE HERCULES
C GONZ CUADRADO
C DE PEDRO MIGUEL
CALLE DE SAN ANA
CALLE ESLAVA
CALLE MEDINA
CALLE PAL MALAVER
CJOAQ COSTA
CALLE DE JUAN RABADAN
DEL GRAN PODER
C ALMTE ESPIN
CALLE CASTELLAR
Conv Sta M la Real
C I CASTILLO LASTRUCCI
C DE PASCUAL DE GAYANGOS
C MIGUEL DEL CID
C DE TEODOSIO
C DE MARTINEZ MONTAÑES
C DE SAN F DE PAULA
CALLE DE JESUS
CALLE TRAJANO
C DEL AMOR DE DIOS
CALLE VIRIATO
S J DE LA PALMA
C ESPIRITU SANTO
C DE SOR ANGELA DE LA CRUZ
Cuartel del Carmen
CALLE DARSENA
CALLE DE GOLES
CALLE DE MENDOZA RIOS
CALLE DE SAN VICENTE
C DE LAVERA CRUZ
CALLE DE BAÑOS
C DE JUAN DE AVILA
CALLE CERVANTES
C DON PEDRO NIÑO
C JER HERNANDEZ
CENTRO
C BAJELES LIÑAN
C REDES
CALLE DABIADO GORDILLO
C JESUS DE LAVERA CRUZ
C TENIENTE BORGES
C DAOIZ
C J GESTOSO
PL DE LA ENCARNACION
Iglesia de San Pedro
CALLE DE ALFONSO XII
CALLE M VILLA
C DE LARAÑA IMAGEN
PL SAN PEDRO
Museo de Bellas Artes
CALLE MONSALVES
CALLE DE SAN ELOY
Iglesia de la Anunciación
PUENTE PELLON
PL CRISTO DE BURGOS
Plaza de Armas
CALLE MARQUES DE PARADAS
CALLE DE PEDRO DEL TORO
CALLE DE CRAVINA
CALLE DE BAILEN
C DE S ROQ
C DE VELILLA
C O'DONNELL
Palacio de Lebrija
C DE LA CUNA
C BOTEROS
AVE DEL CRISTO DE LA EXPIRACION
C GONZ ABREU
Iglesia de la Magdalena
CALLE RIOJA
C DE LAS SIERPES
Iglesia del Salvador
Pte del Cachorro
CALLE CANALEJAS
C DE GRAVINA
CALLE DE SAN PABLO
CALLE MENDE
CALLE VELAZQUEZ
SAGASTA
CALLE SAN ISIDORO
CORRAL DEL REY
Jardines de Chapina
CALLE DE ARJONA
CALLE DE TRASTAMARA
CALLE MORATIN
CALLE DEL CAÑAL
Mon Rom
C BENIDORM
Ayuntamiento
PL NUEVA
C HERN COLON
CALLE DE ADRIANO
C ALMANSA
C DE SANTAS PATRONAS
CALLE ZARAGOZA
C CAMAZO
C ALVAREZ QUINTERO
ARGOTE DE MOLINA
C DE AIRE
Palacio Arzobispal
C DE GUZMAN EL BUENO
CALLE DE CASTILLA
CALLE DE ALFARERIA
C DE PASTOR Y LANDERO
CALLE GALERA
CALLE CASTELAR
C P MARCHENA
EL ARENAL
CALLE DE ADRIANO
CALLE GENIL
Plaza de Toros de la Real Maestranza
Catedral y Giralda
PL V REYES
CALLE DE MATEOS GAGO
Hospital de los Venerables
PTE DE ISABEL II
PL CABILDO
AVENIDA DE LA CONSTITUCION
Archivo de Indias
PL DEL TRIUNFO
SANTA CRUZ
CALLE RODRIGO DE TRIANA
CALLE DE LA PUREZA
CALLE DEL BETIS
Dársena
PASEO MARQUES DE CONTADERO
PASEO DE CRISTOBAL COLON
C VARFLORA
C VELARDE
C DOS DE MAYO
Hermandad de la Caridad
C TOMAS DE IBARRA
STO TOMAS
Reales Alcázares
Palacio de Cultura
CALLE SANTANDER
Jardines de Murillo
Puerto de Indias
POI
Cathedral
Information
Police Station
Airport
Railway Stn
Bus Station
Hospital

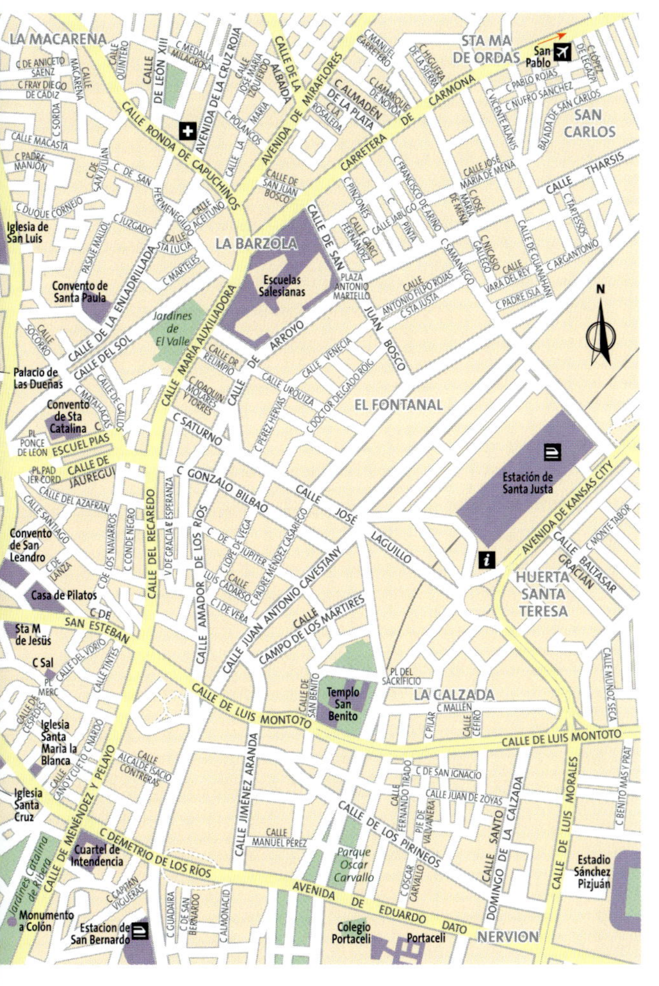

LA MACARENA
STA Mª DE ORDAS
San Pablo
SAN CARLOS
C DE ANICETO SAENZ
C FRAY DIEGO DE CADIZ
CALLE MACARENA
CALLE QUINTERO
CALLE DE LEON XIII
C MEDALLA MILAGROSA
C DE SORDA
CALLE MACASTA
C PADRE MANJON
C DE SAN JULIAN
C DE SAN HERMENEGILDO
AVENIDA DE LA CRUZ ROJA
C JOSE MARIA IZQUIERDO
CALLE LA MARIA
C POLANCOS
CALLE DE MIRAFLORES
CALLE DE LA ALBAIDA
C LA ROSALEDA
C ALMADEN DE LA PLATA
C MANUEL CARRETERO
C HIGUERA DE LA SIERRA
C LAMARQUE DE NOVOA
CARMONA
CARRETERA DE
C PABLO ROJAS
C VICENTE ALANIS
C NUFRO SANCHEZ
BAJADA DE SAN CARLOS
C LOPEZ DE LECAPI
Iglesia de San Luis
CALLE RONDA DE CAPUCHINOS
CALLE ACEITUNO
C DE STA LUCIA
PASAJE MALLOL
C JUZGADO
C MARTELES
LA BARZOLA
CALLE DE SAN JUAN BOSCO
CALLE DE SAN
Escuelas Salesianas
C PINZONES
CALLE CARCI FERNANDEZ
CALLE JABUGO
PINTA
PLAZA ANTONIO MARTELLO
C FRANCISCO DE ARINO
C JOSE MARIA DE MENA
CALLE JOSE MARIA DE MENA
CALLE THARSIS
CALLE TARTESSOS
C NICASIO GALLEGO
C SAMANIEGO
CALLE VARA DEL REY
CALLE DE GUANAHANI
C ARGANTONIO
C PADRE ISLA
CALLE ANTONIO FILPO ROJAS
C STA JUSTA
Convento de Santa Paula
Jardines de El Valle
CALLE DE LA ENLADRILLADA
CALLE DEL SOL
CALLE MARIA AUXILIADORA
CALLE DR RELIMPIO
CALLE DE
ARROYO
CALLE VENECIA
JUAN BOSCO
C DUQUE CORNEJO
CALLE SOCORRO
Palacio de Las Dueñas
C MATAHACAS
CALLE DE GALLOS
C JOAQUIN MORALES Y TORRES
CALLE URQUIZA
C PEREZ HERVAS
C DOCTOR DELGADO ROIG
EL FONTANAL
Convento de Sta Catalina
PL PONCE DE LEON
ESCUEL PIAS
C SATURNO
PL PAD JER CORD
CALLE DE JAUREGUI
CALLE DEL AZAFRAN
CALLE SANTIAGO
C DE LOS NAVARROS
C CONDE NEGRO
CALLE DEL RECAREDO
V DE GRACIA Y ESPERANZA
C GONZALO BILBAO
CALLE DE LOS RIOS
C DE VEGA
C LOPE DE JUPITER
CALLE JOSE
LAGUILLO
Estación de Santa Justa
AVENIDA DE KANSAS CITY
CALLE BALTASAR GRACIAN
C MONTE TABOR
HUERTA SANTA TERESA
Convento de San Leandro
C DE LANZA
LUIS CADARSO
CALLE
C PADRE MENDEZ CASARIEGO
Casa de Pilatos
C DE SAN ESTEBAN
CJ DE VERA
CALLE AMADOR DE LOS RIOS
CALLE JUAN ANTONIO CAVESTANY
CALLE CAMPO DE LOS MARTIRES
Sta M de Jesús
C Sal
CALLE DEL VIDRIO
CALLE TINTES
PL MERC
PL DEL SACRIFICIO
CALLE DE SAN BENITO
Templo San Benito
LA CALZADA
C MALLEN
CALLE MUÑOZ SECA
CALLE DE CESPEDES
CANOY CUETO C NARDO
Iglesia Santa Maria la Blanca
CALLE DE LUIS MONTOTO
C PILAR
CALLE CEFIRO
CALLE DE LUIS MONTOTO
Iglesia Santa Cruz
CALLE DE MENENDEZ Y PELAYO
C DEMETRIO DE LOS RIOS
CALLE JIMENEZ ARANDA
CALLE ALCALDE ISACIO CONTRERAS
C DE SAN IGNACIO
CALLE FERNANDO TIRADO
CALLE JUAN DE ZOYAS
PIE DE VALVANERA
CALLE DE LA CALZADA
CALLE DE LUIS MORALES
C BENITO MAS Y PRAT
Jardines Catalina de Ribera
Cuartel de Intendencia
C CAPITAN VIGUERAS
C GUADAIRA
C DE SAN BERNARDO
CALMONACID
CALLE MANUEL PEREZ
Parque Oscar Carvallo
CALLE DE LOS PIRINEOS
C OSCAR CARVALLO
CALLE SANTO DOMINGO DE LA CALZADA
Estadio Sánchez Pizjuán
Monumento a Colón
Estacion de San Bernardo
AVENIDA DE EDUARDO DATO
Colegio Portaceli
Portaceli
NERVION
N

SEVILLE CARD

The Seville Card gives free admission for one, two or three days to all the major monuments and museums in the city (sometimes with guided tour), Isla Mágica and the zoo. You can use the hop-on-hop-off official Seville Tour bus, take a cruise down the river and, if you pay a little more, have unlimited use of the TUSSAM public bus network. Show the card and you'll get discounts in many restaurants, shops, flamenco shows and clubs. The card can be bought on-line or at any tourist information office ❶ (902) 87 79 96 Ⓦ www.sevillacard.es

A good way to see a lot in a hurry is to take an open-top double-decker tour bus ride with either **SevillaTour** (❶ (902) 10 10 81 Ⓦ www.sevillatour.com 🕐 10.00–18.00 Nov–Mar; 10.00–22.00 Apr–Oct) or **Sevirama Tour por Sevilla** (❶ (954) 56 06 93 Ⓦ www.busturistico.com 🕐 10.00–18.00 Nov–Apr, 10.00–22.00 May–Oct). Although these are advertised as hop-on-hop-off services there are only actually four stops. However, their great advantage is that they enable you to skim through the two fair grounds (1929 and 1992), which aren't as rewarding to visit on foot. The place to pick up these buses is near the Torre del Oro.

Taxis are easily hailed on any main street and not too costly. For a pick up call **Radio Taxi** (❶ (954) 58 00 00) or **Tele Taxi** (❶ (954) 62 22 22). A green light means a taxi is for hire. The fare will be fixed by meter, which may start at a minimum charge. Tariffs increase at night and if you have luggage.

With no hills, Seville is a good city to cycle around. What's more, there are a few dedicated cycle lanes, including a recreational one beside the river near the Plaza de Armas shopping centre. A bicycle can be a good way of exploring the far reaches of the Parque de María Luisa and the Isla de la Cartuja, but it's almost impossible to avoid busy roads. For bicycle hire contact **Cyclotour** stands at either Avenida de Hernán Cortés in Parque de María Luisa (by the Plaza de España, ⏱ from 10.00) or **Paseo Marqués de Contadero**, next to the Torre del Oro (☎ (954) 68 96 66 or (605) 90 26 34 ⓦ www.cyclotouristic.com).

Seville looks different from the river as the traffic noise recedes and you sail under its various bridges. Cruises are operated by **Cruceros Torre del Oro** (ⓐ Alcalde Marqués de Contadero, next to the Torre del Oro ☎ (954) 56 16 92 ⓦ www.crucerostorredeloro.com).

⬥ *Take a taxi from the station – otherwise, it's more fun to walk*

671
935
631
738
931
944
897
834
832
818
(Barqueta)
027
783
222
026
238
818
Puente de
la Barqueta
809
808
(Barqueta)
018
925
019
025
737
936
C1 Barqueta
C2 Barqueta
C3 Barqueta
C4 Barqueta
6
810
237
LA
MACARENA
730
937
C2
C1
729
016
029
13
14
B2
236
SAN
VICENTE
235
938
519
780
781
234
13 14
Plaza Duque
248
510
030
015
960
(Pza del Duque)
563
13
14
554
(Pza Encarnación)
597
Encarnación
B2
718
939
747
745
550
556
555
559
ENCARNACION
Encarnación
32
711
748
509
B2
848
Puente Cristo
de la Expiración
746
Giralda
933
(Puerta Triana)
6
899
779
Pza. Toros de
la Maestranza
940
(Puerta Triana)
013
Puente
de Isabel II
777
557
5
6
775
749
(Paseo de Co
Porta Triana 5
773
012
Marqués del
Contadero Dock
932
(Puerta Triana)
772
884
Betis
Torre
del Oro
771
6
5
231
890
882
010
Puente de
San Telmo
770
C1
768
TRIANA
C3
619
C2
769
958
Los Remedios
B2
396
180
200
5
LOS
REMEDIOS
5
214
957
956
202
203
Gta. S. Lazaro 6
13 P. Montano
14 Pgno. Norte
A Communicarta
Style45 design
© Communicarta Ltd 2007 UDN.1a
Map user Ref:WZFG/CS/SVQ/2007/30

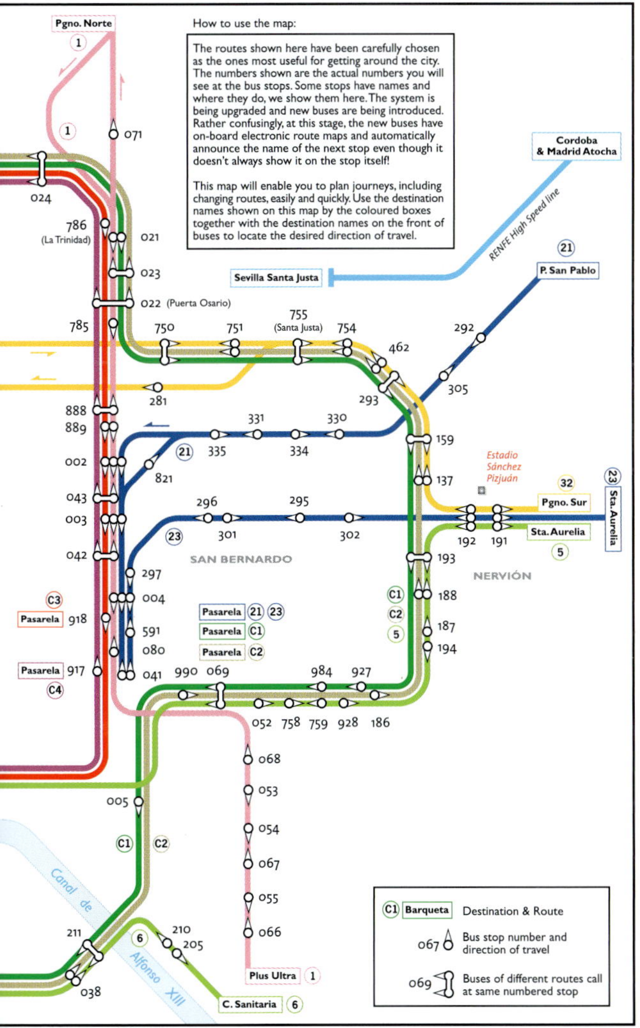

Pgno. Norte
1
1
071
024
786
(La Trinidad)
021
023
022 (Puerta Osario)
785
750
751
755
(Santa Justa)
754
462
281
888
889
331
330
335
334
002
821
043
296
295
003
301
302
042
SAN BERNARDO
297
004
C3
Pasarela
918
591
080
Pasarela
917
041
990
069
984
927
C4
052 758 759 928 186
068
005
053
C1
C2
054
067
055
066
Plus Ultra
1
C. Sanitaria
6
211
6
210
205
038
Canal de
Alfonso XIII
Cordoba
& Madrid Atocha
RENFE High Speed line
21
P. San Pablo
Sevilla Santa Justa
292
305
293
159
137
Estadio
Sánchez
Pizjuán
32
Pgno. Sur
23
Sta. Aurelia
192 191
Sta. Aurelia
5
NERVIÓN
193
C1
188
C2
187
5
194
21
335
21
23
23
301
Pasarela 21 23
Pasarela C1
Pasarela C2

How to use the map:

The routes shown here have been carefully chosen
as the ones most useful for getting around the city.
The numbers shown are the actual numbers you will
see at the bus stops. Some stops have names and
where they do, we show them here. The system is
being upgraded and new buses are being introduced.
Rather confusingly, at this stage, the new buses have
on-board electronic route maps and automatically
announce the name of the next stop even though it
doesn't always show it on the stop itself!

This map will enable you to plan journeys, including
changing routes, easily and quickly. Use the destination
names shown on this map by the coloured boxes
together with the destination names on the front of
buses to locate the desired direction of travel.

C1 Barqueta   Destination & Route
067   Bus stop number and
       direction of travel
069   Buses of different routes call
       at same numbered stop

HORSE-DRAWN CARRIAGES

These exist, of course, purely for tourists but, come the April Fair (see page 12), anyone who is anyone in Seville will be seen driving around Seville at horse-pace. And it is an undeniably leisurely and enjoyable way to get the flavour of the city. ⓐ Drivers wait for fares in the Plaza del Triunfo outside the cathedral, in the Parque de María Luisa (next to the Plaza de España) and near the Torre del Oro

Boats leave every 30 minutes 11.00–23.00 May–Oct;11.00–19.00 Nov–Apr for a one-hour trip to see the historical and modern sights of the city. At weekends from May to September they also sail down to the mouth of the Guadalquivir at Sanlúcar de Barrameda on the edge of Doñana National Park (see page 108).

CAR HIRE

Narrow streets and traffic jams mean it's not worth trying to drive around the city centre. In addition, car parks and parking spaces can be hard to find. If you have arrived by car it is best to leave it parked in a hotel garage or secure car park and explore on foot, public transport or taxi. Three of the most reputable companies who have offices in the city are:

Avis ❶ (902) 13 55 31 Ⓦ www.avis.es

Hertz ❶ (902) 40 24 05 Ⓦ www.hertz.es

National/Atesa ❶ (954) 51 47 35 Ⓦ www.atesa.es

For more information on car hire, see page 145.

---

❶ *Aerial view of Seville with her famous bullring*

THE CITY OF
Seville

Santa Cruz & the city centre

The Barrio de Santa Cruz is the heart and soul of Seville. Indeed if all the allures of southern Spain could be distilled into one neighbourhood of one city, this tangle of picturesque streets, squares and beguiling alleyways would definitely be it.

In many ways, the area is a seamless blend of the authentic and the stereotypical: white houses with details picked out in ochre and crimson, the forbidding iron grilles over their windows offset by pots of flowering geraniums. At every turn there is some pleasant bar or restaurant with outdoor tables ready for breakfast, tapas or a leisurely meal. The main reason why Santa Cruz has survived quite as intact as it has is that there are few streets through it built for cars. The best (but busiest) pedestrian route into Santa Cruz is through the short tunnel in the corner of Patio de Banderas (next to the exit from the Reales Alcázares, see page 66), which leads into Calle Judería, whose name is a reminder that this was once the Jewish quarter of the city.

Santa Cruz proper stretches east from here to Calle Menéndez y Pelayo – this is its picture-postcard core – but it continues northwards to the Casa de Pilatos. Once you are immersed in the labyrinth, a map is not much use, but there are two landmarks to help you. Occasionally you'll catch a glimpse of the Giralda (see page 63), giving you a rough west point; to the south the *barrio* is limited by the gardens of the Reales Alcázares.

Beautiful though it is, after a while Santa Cruz can feel a little claustrophobic. So it can be a relief to discover Seville's agreeable city centre, helpfully known simply as 'Centro'.

Santa Cruz &
the city centre
0   250 metres
0   250 yards
N
CENTRO
EL ARENAL
SANTA CRUZ
CALLE CASTELLAR
C ESPIRITU SANTO
CALLE DE S J DE LA PALMA
Palacio de
Las Duenas
CALLE JER HERNÁNDEZ
CALLE DE SOR ANGELA DE LA CRUZ
CALLE GERONA
CALLE DE BUSTOS TAVERA
CALLE SOCORRO
CALLE DEL SOL
Convento de
Santa Paula
Jardines
de El Valle
C MATAHACAS
CALLE DE GALLOS
Convento
de Sta
Catalina
PLAZA DE
TERCEROS
PL PONCE
DE LEÓN
C ESCUEL PIAS
C DE JÁUREGUI
CALLE TRAJANO
CALLE DEL AMOR DE DIOS
CALLE DAOIZ
C J GESTOSO
PL DE LA
ENCARNACIÓN
Iglesia de
San Pedro
2
PL SAN PEDRO
C ALMIRANTE APODACA
CALLE ALMUDENA
PL PAD JER CORD
C FRANCISCO CARRIÓN MEJIAS
CALLE DEL AZAFRÁN
CALLE SANTIAGO
PL DUQUE
DE LA
VICTORIA
C MARTIN VILLA
C DE LARAÑA IMAGEN
4
Iglesia de la
Anunciación
Palacio de la
Condesa de
Lebrija
PUENTE Y PELLO
CALLE DE LA CUNA
PL CRISTO
DE BURGOS
CALLE BOTEROS
C DE ALHÓNDIGA
Convento
de San
Leandro
C DE LANZA
CALLE IMPERIAL
C O'DONNELL
CALLE RIOJA
C DE MUÑOZ
MUÑOZ OLIVE
CALLE DE LAS SIERPES
CALLE VELAZQUEZ
3
PLAZA DE
SALVADOR
C SAGASTA
CALLE SIETE REVUELTAS
11
8
C PÉREZ GALDÓS
PL ALFALFA
PL
ALFALFA
Casa de
Pilatos
CALLE AGUILAS
CALLE DE LOS NAVARROS
CALLE CONDE NEGRO
CALLE DEL RECAREDO
17
C MENDEZ
12
Iglesia del
Salvador
CALLE CUESTA
DEL ROSARIO
Museo
del Baile
Flamenco
Sta M
de Jesús
CALLE DE SAN ESTEBAN
CALLE DEL VORIO
7
CALLE SAN
ISIDORO
CALLE CORRAL DEL REY
CALLE DON REMONDO
C SAL
PL DES
FRANCISCO
PL
NUEVA
Ayuntamiento
CALLE PAJARITOS
10
Mon
Rom
CALLE MÁRMOLES
C MUÑOZ Y PABÓN
SAN JOSÉ
PL MERC
CALLE ZARAGOZA
7
CALLE DE ALVAREZ QUINTERO
C DE FRANCOS
C HERN COLON
18
C DE ARGOTE DE MOLINA
CALLE DEL AIRE
1
CALLE DE LEVIES
STA MARIA LA BLANCA
CALLE DE CÉSPEDES
Iglesia
Santa Maria
la Blanca
C GAMAZO
Catedral
y Giralda
PL
CABILDO
AVENIDA DE LA CONSTITUCIÓN
Palacio
Arzobispal
CALLE DE GUZMAN
EL BUENO
Iglesia
Santa
Cruz
CALLE FARNESIO
9
PLV
REYES
C DE MATEOS GAGO
CALLE XIMÉNEZ DE ENCISO
C DE STA TERESA
PLAZA
REFINADORES
C CANO Y CUETO
15
C DE MENÉNDEZ Y PELAYO
C DEMETRIO DE LOS RÍOS
C GARCIA DE VINUESA
5
C TOMÁS DE IBARRA
PL DEL
TRIUNFO
6
Hospital
de los
Venerables
PLAZA DE LOS
VENERABLES
16
PL
STA CRUZ
Cuartel de
Intendencia
CALLE DE CIFUENTES
CALLE CAPITAN VIGUERAS
Hermandad
de la Caridad
Archivo General
de Indias
CALLE STO TOMÁS
14
13
CALLEJÓN DEL AGUA
CALLE DEL AGUA
CALLEJÓN DE RUEDA
C DOS DE MAYO
CALLE TEMPRADO
Palacio de
Cultura
C SANTANDER
C HABANA
Reales
Alcázares
PLAZA
CONTRATACION
C JUDERIA
SANTA
CRUZ
Monumento
a Colón
Jardines Catalina
de Ribera
Estacion de
San Bernardo
AVENIDA DE CADIZ
PLAZA DE SAN
GREGORIO
CALLE
MARIANA
DE PINEDA
Jardines
de Murillo
AVENIDA DE
MALAGA
PUERTA
DE JEREZ
ALMIRANTE LOBO
SAN FERNANDO
19
Palacio
de Justicia
PLAZA
DE S SEBASTIAN
El Prado de
San Sebastián
Torre del Oro
Museo Maritimo
AVE DE
SANJURJO
Jardines
de Cristina
Hotel
Alfonso XIII
DOÑA MARIA DE PADILLA
PLAZA DON
JUAN DE
AUSTRIA
JOSE MA OSBORNE
PTE S TELMO
AVE DE ROMA
Palacio de
San Telmo
Jardines
de San Telmo
Universidad
AVENIDA DE PORTUGAL
POI
Cathedral
Information
Police Station
Airport
Railway Stn
Bus Station
Hospital

SIGHTS & ATTRACTIONS

Casa de Pilatos

This aristocratic palace dates from the late 15th and early 16th centuries and speaks of Seville at its most wealthy and powerful. It was named 'the House of Pontius Pilate' after one of its early owners, Don Fadrique, the first Marquis of Tarifa, returned from the Holy Land in 1519 and discovered that the distance between it and a local shrine was the same as that between the supposed site of the Praetorium (where Christ was condemned to death) in Jerusalem and Golgotha (where he was crucified).

The tranquil, shady gardens of the Casa de Pilatos

The house, owned by the Dukes of Medinaceli and administered on their behalf by a foundation, is in a mixture of Gothic, Mudéjar (derived from Islamic architecture) and Italian Renaissance styles. It has a number of interesting decorative features including coffered ceilings, paintings, furniture, classical statues, frescoes and a marvellous dome over the main staircase. The walls around the two-storey central patio are worth seeing (even if you ignore the rest of the building), as they are covered with old tiles in a glorious clash of colours and styles. Outside, the Renaissance gardens are worth seeing, too. ⓐ Pl. de Pilatos 1 ❶ (954) 22 52 98 ❶ 09.00–18.00 Jan & Feb, Sept–Dec; 09.00–19.00 Mar–Aug. Admission charge (free on Tues ❶ 13.00–17.00)

Catedral y Giralda

'We'll build a church that will make anyone who looks at it think we were mad,' the city fathers are supposed to have said in the early 14th century as they set out to build Seville's great cathedral. The building took over a century to complete and the result was, and is, the largest Gothic building in Europe.

It stands on the site of a 12th-century mosque, and the only surviving remains of the original building are the cloister of the Patio de los Naranjos ('Courtyard of the Orange Trees', which was used for ritual ablutions by Muslim worshippers) and the Giralda Tower, formerly a minaret, which looms above the cathedral as the city's unmistakable landmark.

Inside, five aisles divided into nine sections each, and flanked by 20 chapels, create a massive floor space. The focal point is inevitably the high altar with its great altarpiece, one of the largest in the world, made of gold panels carved in relief by Flemish and Spanish artists. Other features to look out for are the Royal Chapel, the

◔ *The Giralda Tower soars over Seville's massive Gothic cathedral*

138 stained-glass windows and the ornate tomb of at least some of Christopher Columbus (see opposite).

The highlight of the visit, however, is a walk up the 104-m-high (341-ft) Giralda Tower. The tower has a series of ramps running up the middle of it which once allowed horses or mules to be ridden to the top.

The tower is actually an ingenious bit of architectural grafting as it is one tower superimposed on another. The bottom two-thirds are a brick-built minaret; the upper part is a stone-and-brick Renaissance

THE MYSTERY OF COLUMBUS'S TOMB

Christopher Columbus has travelled almost as much since he's been dead as he did when he was alive. When he handed in his passport for good (or so you might reasonably have thought), in Valladolid on 20 May 1506, he was initially buried in a cemetery in the city. But three years later his family had the corpse taken to Seville where his eldest son, Diego, was buried beside him in 1526. Seville was, of course, of great significance to Columbus, as it was from here that he set off on the journey that would eventually lead him to America. But Diego's widow insisted on having both bodies moved to Santo Domingo on the Caribbean island of Hispaniola, claiming that that's what Christopher would have wanted. But his resting in peace here was disturbed by international events. When the French threatened to capture Hispaniola in 1795, a worried Spain had his remains transferred for safe keeping to Havana, Cuba. A century later, Cuba gained its independence and Columbus was again relocated to his final resting place in Seville cathedral.

Or was he? Rumours have abounded for years that Christopher never actually made it back to Seville. Certainly, each time he was moved (or was supposed to have been), there was the possibility of an embarrassing mistake being made, and there is some evidence that it was the body of Diego that was (erroneously) moved to Havana. This would have meant that Christopher Columbus stayed buried in Santo Domingo in the Dominican Republic. However, DNA tests in 2006 proved that at least some of Columbus's remains are in the tomb in Seville. Some? So where's the rest of him?

belfry added in 1568. On the pinnacle of the spire stands a weathervane: a bronze figure of Faith popularly known as 'El Giraldillo' from which the tower derives its name. ⓐ Pl. Virgen de los Reyes (Puerta del Lagarto) ⓣ (954) 21 49 71 Ⓦ www.catedralsevilla.org Ⓛ 11.00–17.00 Sept–June; 09.30–16.00 Jul & Aug. Admission charge (free on Sun)

Reales Alcázares

What makes this royal pad (the King stays here when he's in town) special is the way in which Muslim architectural styles have been fused with Christian ones. The core of the Alcazar is the Mudéjar Palace (also called the Palacio de Don Pedro), which was created by Pedro I (the Cruel) between 1364 and 1366. To fulfil his plans he sent to Córdoba and Granada for the best Muslim craftsmen working in his day.

The complex is entered by the Puerta del León, which leads into the Patio del León. One room to the left is the Patio del Yeso (Patio of the Plaster), the only bit of the Almohad Palace still intact.

From the Patio del León you step into the Patio de la Montería, the fulcrum of the complex where the court used to assemble for hunting expeditions. Directly in front of you is the façade of the Mudéjar Palace. But before you enter it, have a look at the audience chamber, or Casa de Contratación, to the right. Against one wall here is the *Altarpiece of the Navigators*, painted in 1531–6 and almost certainly the first work of art to depict the discovery of the Americas. In its central panel the Virgin Mary spreads her cape protectively over an assembly of discoverers and *conquistadores*.

The finest room of the palace is the Salón de los Embajadores (Hall of the Ambassadors), which is noticeable for its great dome – a complex geometric arrangement of interlocking gold-painted wood.

Also worth seeing are the Patio de las Muñecas (Patio of the Dolls) named after the two small faces that adorn one of its arches,

Moorish designs in the courtyard of the Reales Alcázares

and the Patio de las Doncellas (Patio of the Maidens), with its superb plasterwork. North of the Mudéjar Palace you pass into the Salones de Carlos V, sumptuous, Gothic-vaulted apartments and a chapel added on the orders of the eponymous monarch. Behind the palace is a large triangle of delightful walled gardens. ⓐ Patio de Banderas ⓣ (954) 50 23 23 ⓦ www.patronato-alcazarsevilla.es ⓛ 09.30–19.00 Tues–Sat, 09.30–17.00 Sun, Apr–Sept; 09.30–17.00 Tues–Sat, 09.30–13.30 Sun, Oct–Mar; closed Mon. Admission charge

CULTURE

Archivo General de Indias

This immense depository of the records of imperial Spain's centuries of colonialism occupies a 16th-century building. In the 18th century King Carlos III decided to use it to archive in one place the vast store of documents relating to Spain's New World possessions. It is still a working library consulted by scholars from all over the world. Its 8 km (5 miles) of shelves hold 43,000 files and more than 80 million pages of original documents – including Columbus's journal. ⓐ Av. de la Constitución 3 ⓣ (954) 21 12 34 ⓦ www.mcu.es/archivos/visitas/index.html ⓛ 09.00–15.45 Mon–Sat, 10.00–13.45 Sun

Museo del Baile Flamenco (Flamenco Museum)

This museum aims to present flamenco as a mainstream art form. There's a gift-shop selling various flamenco-related items, plus evening concerts. If you are here for long enough, you can even take flamenco dance classes. ⓐ C/ Manuel Rojas Marcos 3, near Pl. Alfalfa ⓣ (954) 34 03 11 ⓦ www.museoflamenco.com ⓛ 09.30–18.00. Admission charge

Palacio de la Condesa de Lebrija

This 16th-century Renaissance-Mudéjar palace could be considered the city's alternative archaeological museum. Among many other items is one of the finest mosaics from the Roman remains of Itálica (see page 109). Upstairs are the living quarters of the eponymous countess. ⓐ C/ Cuna 8 ⓣ (954) 22 78 02 ⓦ www.palaciodelebrija.com ⓛ 10.00–13.00, 17.00–19.30 Mon–Fri, 10.00–13.00 Sat, Apr–Nov; 10.00–13.00, 16.30–19.00 Mon–Fri, 10.00–13.00 Sat, May–Oct, closed Sun. Admission charge

RETAIL THERAPY

Centro's best shops are concentrated along Calle Sierpes and Tetuán/Velázquez, which run between Plaza Nueva/Plaza San Francisco and Plaza Campana/Plaza del Duque de la Victoria.

Adolfo Domínguez Spanish designer known especially for his men's suits and shoes. ⓐ Sierpes 2 ⓣ (954) 22 65 38 ⓦ www.adolfodominguez.com ⓛ 10.15–14.00, 17.00–20.30 Mon–Sat, closed Sun

La Alacena Real Old grocer's-cum-delicatessen selling fine wines, olive oils, cheeses, hams and other fine Spanish foods. Any product can be vacuum packed on the premises for safe transport home. ⓐ Pajaritos 11 ⓣ (954) 22 00 90 ⓛ 11.00–15.00, 18.00–22.00 Mon–Fri, 11.00–15.00 Sat, closed Sun

Casa Rodriguez Statues of saints, icons and sundry religious objects. ⓐ Francos 35 ⓣ (954) 22 78 42 ⓛ 10.00–13.30, 17.00–20.30 Mon–Fri, 10.00–14.00 Sat, closed Sun

Compás Sur Mainly a place to buy recordings of flamenco, this shop will also set you up with flamenco guitar or dance classes. ⓐ Cuesta del Rosario 7E, between Pl. del Alfalfa and Pl. de Salvador ⓣ (954) 21 56 62 ⓦ www.compas-sur.com ⓛ 10.30–14.30, 17.30–22.00 Mon–Fri, 10.30–14.30 Sat, closed Sun

El Corte Inglés Spain's leading department store, on eight floors with a restaurant and supermarket stocked with delicacies. ⓐ Pl. del Duque de la Victoria 8 ⓣ (954) 59 70 00 ⓦ www.elcorteingles.com ⓛ 10.00–22.00 Mon–Sat, closed Sun

Flamenco Cool If you're secretly fantasising over all those lurid colours and flouncy dresses, this is the shop for you. Dancing shoes with wings, over-the-top candles, postmodern bullfighters' capes and spots to create your own flamenco bling. ⓐ Amor de Dios 14 ⓣ (954) 91 51 94 ⓦ www.flamencocool.com ⓛ 10.00–14.30, 17.30–21.00 Mon–Fri, 11.00–14.30, 18.00–21.30 Sat, closed Sun

Explore the narrow shopping streets near the cathedral

Mango There are five branches of this chain selling fashion for the young, urban woman in Seville. ⓐ Velazquez 7 ⓣ (954) 22 33 89 ⓦ www.mango.es ⓛ 10.00–21.00 Mon–Sat, closed Sun

Sevillarte A ceramics and handicraft centre selling traditional and new designs. Also stocks Lladró porcelain (made in Valencia). ⓐ Sierpes 66 ⓣ (954) 21 28 36 ⓦ www.sevillarte.com ⓛ 10.00–13.30, 17.30–21.00 Mon–Fri, 10.00–14.30 Sat, closed Sun

Victorio y Lucchino A world-renowned fashion duo who started their business in Seville in the 1970s and are still based here. Their bold and colourful designs have an unmistakeably Andaluz feel. ⓐ Pl. Nueva 10 ⓣ (954) 50 26 60 ⓦ www.victorioylucchino.com ⓛ 10.00–20.30 Mon–Sat, closed Sun

Zara A Spanish institution because of its affordable fashion for women, men and children. ⓐ Pl. del Duque de la Victoria 1 ⓣ (954) 21 48 75 ⓦ www.zara.com ⓛ 10.00–20.30 Mon–Sat, closed Sun

TAKING A BREAK

CAFÉS & ICE CREAMS

Aire de Sevilla £ ❶ A Moroccan-style *teteria* (tea room) near the cathedral, with trickling fountains, colourful fabrics and an extensive list of juices and teas. ⓐ Aire 15 ⓣ (955) 01 00 25 ⓛ 10.00–00.00

Heladería Rayas £ ❷ Seville's most renowned ice cream shop, with a range of wonderful home-made flavours, from gazpacho to olive oil. ⓐ Almirante Apodaca 1 (Pl. de San Pedro) ⓣ (954) 22 17 46 ⓛ 10.00–22.00

Ochoa £ ❸ An old cake shop and tea room which serves home-made ice creams and claims to serve the best milkshakes in Seville. ⓐ Sierpes 45 ⓣ (954) 22 55 28 ⓛ 10.00–21.00

Confitería La Campana ££ ❹ Seville's oldest café-cum-cake shop: a landmark on the square of the same name at the end of Calle Sierpes. ⓐ C/ Sierpes 1–3 ⓣ (954) 22 35 70 ⓛ 08.00–22.00 Mon–Fri, 08.00–23.00 Sat & Sun

TAPAS & BARS

Casa Morales £ ❺ The city's second-oldest bar, and a good place to eat tapas and taste wines. ⓐ García de Vinuesa 11 ⓣ (954) 22 12 42 ⓛ 12.00–16.00, 20.00–00.00

Casa Román £ ❻ A dusty local bar, with great tapas and tables outside in a peaceful, sunny square. The speciality is excellent *jamón ibérico*. ⓐ Pl. de los Venerables 1 ⓣ (954) 22 84 83 ⓛ 09.00–16.00, 19.30–00.00 Mon–Sat, 09.30–16.00 Sun

Entrecárceles £ ❼ Sophisticated, award-winning tapas are served with a variety of vintage wines and sherries in this handsome little bar. ⓐ Faisanes 1 (off Plaza San Francisco) ⓛ 12.00–16.00, 19.00–00.00

Europa £ ❽ Come here for tapas at any time of day or an early breakfast that's hearty and good value. ⓐ Siete Revueltas 35 ⓣ (954) 22 13 54 ⓦ www.bareuropa.info ⓛ 08.00–01.00

Cervecería Giralda ££ ❾ Exquisite tapas including mushroom and cod pie, stuffed courgettes, sirloin stuffed with ham, egg and parsley, and 'Seville's most famous stuffed peppers'. ⓐ Mateos Gago 1 ❶ (954) 22 74 35 🕐 09.00–00.00 Mon–Sat, 10.00–00.00 Sun

La Estrella ££ ❿ Long-standing bar famed for its award-winning aubergine covered with fried tomatoes, peppers, onions, chopped prawns, hard boiled egg and bechamel sauce and served *au gratin*. ⓐ Estrella 3, near Argote de Molina ❶ (954) 22 75 35 🕐 09.00–00.00 Mon–Sat, closed Sun

AFTER DARK

RESTAURANTS

La Habanita £ ⓫ Cuban food including vegan and vegetarian options. ⓐ Golfo 3, near Pl. Alfalfa ❶ (954) 22 02 02 ⓦ www.habanita.es 🕐 12.30–16.30, 20.00–23.00 Mon–Sat, 12.30–16.30 Sun

La Alicantina ££ ⓬ Bar and restaurant in which the menu is especially strong on fish and seafood. Large terrace. Vegetarians catered for. ⓐ Pl. del Salvador 2 ❶ (954) 22 61 22 🕐 12.00–00.00 Mon–Sat, closed Sun, Jul & Aug; 12.00–00.00 Mon–Sat, 12.00–17.00 Sun, Sept–June

Corral del Agua ££ ⓭ Despite its position in the heart of touristville, Corral del Agua maintains its high standards of local cooking. Ask for a table on its leafy patio, where a fountain gurgles gently. ⓐ Callejón del Agua 6 ❶ (954) 22 48 41 🕐 12.30–23.00

Hostería del Laurel £𝐟 ⓮ Supposedly the place where Zorillo was inspired to write *Don Juan Tenorio*. A good place for tapas or a full meal at outdoor tables in one of Santa Cruz's picturesque squares. Also a hotel (see page 36). ⓐ Pl. de los Venerables 5 ⓣ (954) 22 02 95 ⓦ www.hosteriadellaurel.com ⓛ 11.00–16.00, 20.00–00.00

La Judería £𝐟 ⓯ Highly rated restaurant for a special lunch or night out. Traditional Andalucian cuisine and a large selection of wines. ⓐ Cano y Cueto 13 ⓣ (954) 42 64 56 ⓦ www.modestorestaurantes.com ⓛ 13.00–17.00, 19.30–00.30

La Albahaca £££ ⓰ Atmospheric and elegant restaurant in a beautiful old 1920s house. ⓐ Pl. Santa Cruz 12 ⓣ (954) 22 07 14 ⓦ www.andalunet.com/la-albahaca ⓛ 12.00–16.00, 20.00–00.00 Mon–Sat, closed Sun

Becerrita £££ ⓱ Sevillian cuisine and tapas. ⓐ Recaredo 9 (Puerta Carmona) ⓣ (954) 41 20 57 ⓛ 12.30–16.30, 20.00–00.30 Mon–Sat, 12.30–16.30 Sun

Casa Robles £££ ⓲ A chain of four establishments, including a tapas bar. ⓐ Álvarez Quintero 58 ⓣ (954) 21 31 50 ⓦ www.roblesrestaurantes.com ⓛ 13.00–18.00, 21.00–01.00

Egāna-Oriza £££ ⓳ Usually classed as Seville's top restaurant. The cuisine is a fusion of Basque and Andalucian. ⓐ San Fernando 41 ⓣ (954) 22 72 11 ⓦ www.restauranteoriza.com ⓛ 13.30–15.30, 21.00–23.30 Mon–Fri, 21.00–23.30 Sat, closed Sun

FLAMENCO SHOWS

Casa de la Memoría de Al Andalus A well-respected centre for the study of Andalucian culture. ⓐ Ximénez de Enciso 28 ⓣ (954) 56 06 70 ⓦ www.casadelamemoria.com ⓛ Show at 21.00

Los Gallos Claims to keep it simple and authentic. ⓐ Pl. de Santa Cruz 11 ⓣ (954) 21 69 81 ⓦ www.tablaolosgallos.com ⓛ Shows (lasting two hours) at 20.00 & 22.30

El Palacio del Embrujo Andaluz Dinner plus a flamenco show make for an expensive night out. If you're counting your pennies swap dinner for a drink. ⓐ Av. María Auxiliadora 18 ⓣ (954) 53 47 20 ⓦ www.elpalacioandaluz.com ⓛ Shows at 19.00 & 20.45

CLUBS & BARS

La Carbonería This bar in the premises of a former coal merchant is a well-known place to hear and see flamenco. ⓐ Levies 18 ⓣ (954) 21 44 60 or 22 99 45 ⓛ 20.00–03.30

Catedral One of the few clubs in the city centre, this one plays on a religious theme. The music is mainly hip hop, house and R&B. ⓐ Cuesta del Rosario 12 ⓣ (954) 21 90 29 ⓛ 16.00–01.00 Mon–Wed, 16.00–03.00 Thur–Sun

El Garlochí The definitive Seville nightlife experience, a visit to El Garlochí involves sipping on the red house cocktail, surrounded by baroque ecclesiastical clutter. Unmissable. ⓐ C/ Boteros 26 ⓛ 18.00–03.00 Tues–Sun, closed Mon

Beyond the centre

To the north, Santa Cruz merges into the large workaday district of La Macarena, bordered to the west by the wide boulevard Alameda de Hércules. There are several churches here, but the only real sight is the basilica of La Macarena (see below), which stands next to a surviving stretch of the city walls.

Head towards the river from Santa Cruz and the cathedral, on the other hand, and you are immediately in El Arenal, the former docksides. Here are two of the city's most distinctive monuments: the bullring (see page 81) and the Torre del Oro (see page 82). Follow the river and you will come to another interesting area of sightseeing: the vast area of greenery which is the Parque de María Luisa (see page 79). East from Santa Cruz, across Calle de Menendez y Pelayo, the sights vanish, but you might well be drawn to this modern part of the city by its growing number of shops, bars and nightspots.

SIGHTS & ATTRACTIONS

Basílica de la Macarena

Seville has always had a strong cult of the Virgin Mary. It has two rival statues of the mother of Jesus which are ceremoniously brought out during the Holy Week processions. One of them resides in Triana. The other, possibly more famous, is housed here in this baroque church built in 1949. The statue was carved in the late 17th century, probably by the sculptress Luisa Roldán (or La Roldana), and its expression is said to be something between a smile and sadness. There's a museum dedicated to the Virgin de la Macarena and the Brotherhood, which maintains her cult as well

Beyond the centre
POI
Cathedral
Information
Police Station
Airport
Railway Stn
Bus Station
Hospital
0   250 metres
0   250 yards
Cartuja '93
Jardines del Guadalquivir
Auditorio
DE LOS DESCABRIMIENTOS
CAMINO
Meandro de San Jerónimo
Convento de San Clemente
C RESOLANA
CALLE BÉCQUER
Torre de los Perdigones
City Walls
Basílica de La Macarena
LA MACARENA
CALLE DE LEÓN XII
CALLE DE LA ALBAIDA
AVENIDA DE LA CRUZ ROJA
AVENIDA DE MIRAFLORES
Convento de Santa Clara
CALLE DE SANTA CLARA
CALLE LUMBRERAS
C DEL PERAL
C DE LA FERIA
CALLE DE RELATOR
CALLE SAN LUIS
C RONDA DE CAPUCHINOS
CARRETERA DE CARMONA
Cuartel del Carmen
Conv Sta M la Real
C Reparad
C ALCOY
CALLE DE SAN VICENTE
CALLE DE SANTA ANA
CALLE DE JUAN RABADÁN
C MATA
ALAMEDA DE HÉRCULES
DEL GRAN PODER
CALLE DE LA FERIA
Iglesia de San Luis
Convento de Santa Paula
Escuelas Salesianas
CALLE DE JESUS
CALLE DE SAN VICENTE
CALLE DEL TORNEO
CALLE TRAJANO
CALLE DEL AMOR DE DIOS
CALLE CASTELLAR
Palacio de Las Dueñas
C DE LA ENLADRILLADA
Jardines de El Valle
C SATURNO
Estación de Santa Justa & Nervión Plaza
CALLE DE San DE BANOS
CENTRO
PL DE LA ENCARNACIÓN
C GERONA
PLAZA DE STA TERCEROS
Convento de Sta Catalina
ESCUEL PIAS
C AMADOR DE LOS RÍOS
CALLE MARÍA AUXILIADORA
CALLE DE ARROYO
CALLE DE RECAREDO
CALLE GONZALO BILBAO
CALLE JOSÉ LAGUILLO
Plaza de Armas
Museo de Bellas Artes
CALLE DE ALFONSO XII
C M VILLAC DE LARAÑA IMAGEN
Iglesia de San Pedro
PL PAD IER CORD
CALLE DE JÁUREGUI
CALLE DE SATURNO
C MARQUES
C DE SAN ELOY
C O'DONNELL
Palacio de Lebrija
Iglesia de la Anunciación
PL SAN PEDRO
PL CRISTO DE BURGOS
C ALHONDIGA
Convento de San Leandro
AVE DEL CRISTO DE LA EXPIRACIÓN
CALLE DE BAILEN
CALLE RIOJA
Iglesia del Salvador
CALLE DEL REY
Casa de Pilatos
C DE SAN ESTEBAN
CALLE JUAN ANTONIO CAVESTANY
CALLE DE PARADAS
CALLE DE SAN PABLO
CALLE VELÁZQUEZ
CORRAL DEL REY
Sta M de Jesús
C Sal
Templo San Benito
Jardines de Chapina
CALLE DE ARJONA
PL NUEVA
CALLE ZARAGOZA
Ayuntamiento
Mon Rom
PL MERC
CALLE DE LUIS MONTOTO
ALMANSA
C PASTOR Y LANDERO
CALLE CAMAZO
EL ARENAL
Palacio Arzobispal
Iglesia Santa María la Blanca
CALLE DE MENÉNDEZ Y PELAYO
Parque Oscar Carvalló
TRIANA
PTE DE ISABEL II
Plaza de Toros de la Real Maestranza
CALLE DE ADRIANO
AVE DE LA CONSTITUCIÓN
Catedral y Giralda
PL V REYES
Iglesia Santa Cruz
Hospital de los Venerables
SANTA CRUZ
CALLE DEMETRIO DE LOS RÍOS
CALLE JIMÉNEZ ARANDA
AVENIDA DE EDUARDO DATO
CALLE DE SAN JACINTO
PASEO DE CRISTÓBAL
Dársena
CALLE DEL BETIS
CALLE ROIO
Hermandad de la Caridad
Archivo de Indias
PL DEL TRIUNFO
Reales Alcázares
Cuartel de Intendencia
Estación de San Bernardo
Estadio Sánchez Pizjuán
PAGES DEL CORRO
PASEO MARQUES
Palacio de Cultura
PL CABILDO
Jardines de Murilo
Jardines Catalina de Ribera
Monumento a Colón
El Prado de San Sebastián
FARMACÉUTICO E M HERRERA
Torre del Oro Museo Maritimo
CALLE SANTANDER
PTE S TELMO
C SAN FERNANDO
Hotel Alfonso XIII
AVE DE CARLOS V
CALLE DE ENRAMADILLA
AVENIDA DE LA REPÚBLICA ARGENTINA
CALLE DEL CONTADERO
Palacio de San Telmo
PALOS DE LA FRONTERA
Universidad
AVENIDA DE PORTUGAL
DR PEDRO CASTRO
LOS REMEDIOS
CALLE DE LA ASUNCIÓN
CALLE DEL MONTE CARMELO
Plaza de España
Parque
PTE DEL GENARALISMO
PRESID CARRERO BLANCO
AVE SANTIAGO MONTOTO
LAS DELICIAS
de
Maria
Luisa
BORBOLLA
Cuartel de Ingenieros
SAN SALVADOR
Museo de Artes y Costumbres Populares
Museo Arqueológico
CALLE DE FELIPE II
C GENERAL MERRY
N
AVE DE M LUISA
AVENIDA DE

as a shop selling devotional items. ⓐ C/ Bécquer 1 ⓣ (954) 90 18 00
ⓦ www.hermandaddelamacarena.es ⓛ Museum 09.30–14.00,
17.00–20.00, closed one week in Lent

Hermandad de la Caridad

Still housing a hospice and community of nuns, this baroque
former almshouse was founded in the 17th century by Miguel
de Mañara, popularly believed to have been the inspiration for
Don Juan. Legend has it that he renounced his life of sin after
a vision of his own death, though versions vary. Whatever the
case, as a former member of the aristocracy he was able to use
his contacts to secure some wonderful paintings for the chapel,
including six by his friend Bartolomé Esteban Murillo and two
stunning works by Juan de Valdés Léal. ⓐ Calle Temprado 3
ⓣ (954) 22 32 32 ⓦ www.santa-caridad.org ⓛ 9am–1.30pm,
3.30–6.30pm Mon–Fri, 9am–1.30pm Sat & Sun; Admission charge

Hotel Alfonso XIII

Seville's premier guesthouse is thought to be the only hotel ever
commissioned by a reigning monarch, having been built on the
orders of Alfonso XIII for heads of state visiting the 1929 Ibero-
American exhibition. He is lucky to have been immortalised in
the name of such a place, as in real life he was not so fortunate.
His insensitive meddling in political and military affairs forced him
to abdicate in 1931 and go into exile. The hotel is in neo-Moorish
style with a central courtyard, sumptuous salons, grand corridors,
an ornate lift, elegant stained-glass panels, crystal chandeliers
and many other exquisite decorative touches. ⓐ San Fernando 2
ⓣ (954) 91 70 00 (see page 39)

Parque de María Luisa & the Plaza de España

In 1929 the city of Seville decided to transform a swathe of the grounds of the 17th-century Palacio de San Telmo into a fairground for the Ibero-American exhibition, a grand venture that didn't quite pay off at the time because the world was heading for depression – this was the year of the Wall Street Crash – but which bequeathed the city some extraordinary architecture as well as a superb park.

In particular, the Plaza de España is Seville at its extravagant, monumental best: a large semicircle of arcades ending in two mock baroque towers borrowed from the pilgrimage city of Santiago de Compostela in northern Spain. But what makes the Plaza de España shine, literally, are its ceramics. Following the curve of the building on the lowest level are technicoloured tiled benches representing the provinces of Spain in alphabetical order. The banisters of the bridges across its canal, meanwhile, are mini-masterpieces of the ceramicist's art.

⬥ *Exuberant ceramics at the Plaza de España*

Plaza de Toros de la Real Maestranza

Built in 1761, Seville's bullring is one of the oldest in Spain and certainly the most famous in the world. The bullring is owned by the Real Maestranza de Caballería (the Royal Corps of the Order of Chivalry of Seville), an organisation created around the time of the Reconquest to prepare and arm mounted knights for battle. It is a curious structure, not circular as might be expected but an irregular polygon made up of 30 sides of varying lengths with a white and ochre vernacular baroque façade looking onto the river bank. A capacity crowd is 13,934 spectators.

The arena itself is egg-shaped with the ground in it slightly higher in the centre than at the edges. Around the ring are all the facilities needed by the world of bullfighting: rooms for the *toreros* (toreadors) and their teams, a chapel (bullfighters are invariably deeply pious), infirmary, bull pens, a 'skinnery' (where dead bulls' hides are removed) and so on. The 20-minute guided visit takes in the highlights of the complex and the museum. This contains *trajes de luces* ('suits of lights' – the bullfighters' stunning outfits), paintings, bulls' heads and other bullfighting treasures.

The bullfighting season traditionally begins on Easter Sunday and ends in October. If you want to attend, there is a bewildering choice of seats. The cheapest are the top *gradas* in full sun (*sol*); the most expensive are those close to the ring in the shade (*sombra*). ⓐ Paseo de Cristóbal Colón 18 ⓣ (954) 22 45 77 For tickets to see a bullfight (954) 50 13 82 or 56 07 59 ⓦ www.realmaestranza.com ⓛ Museum 09.30–19.00 (closes at 15.00 on bullfight days)

◀ The grand entrance of Spain's oldest bullring

Torre del Oro

There's not much to this short, 12-sided tower on the banks of the River Guadalquivir north of the Puente de San Telmo, but it is still a well-known landmark. It was built in the 13th century by the Almohad rulers of southern Spain as part of their defences for the city. Why exactly it is called 'the Tower of Gold' is anyone's guess; at various times in its history it has served as wharf building, lighthouse, prison and chapel. Currently, it is a naval museum. ⓐ Paseo de Cristóbal Colón ⓣ (954) 22 24 19 ⓛ 10.00–14.00 Tues–Fri, 11.00–14.00 Sat & Sun, closed Mon. Admission charge (free on Tues)

Torre de los Perdigones

Once part of an ammunitions factory, this 45-metre (147-ft) tower was where the lead pellets (*perdigones*) were made. The factory was later turned into a park, but the tower has had a camera obscura added for a fascinating and unique view of Seville. It opened to the public in 2007. ⓐ C/ Resolana s/n ⓣ (902) 10 10 81 ⓦ www.torredelosperdigones.com ⓛ 10.00–14.30, 17.00–20.30. Admission charge

Universidad (Royal Tobacco Factory)

One of the most prized discoveries of the New World was tobacco and the majority of Europe's cigarettes were produced here in this vast, palatial factory building, which was completed in 1771 and now serves as part of Seville University. It can be hard to imagine the lives of the 3,000 female workers, *cigarreras*, who spent long working days rolling cigarettes on their thighs. Indeed, we probably wouldn't give them a second thought had they not inspired the world's most enduring musical (see page 86). ⓐ San Fernando ⓣ (954) 55 10 00 ⓦ www.universidaddesevilla.es ⓛ 09.00–21.00 Mon–Fri, closed Sat & Sun

The 13th-century Torre del Oro stands on the banks of the Guadalquivir

CULTURE

Museo Arqueológico & Museo de Artes y Costumbres Populares

At the far end of the Parque de María Luisa from the city, two museums face each other across the Plaza de América, both of them occupying pavilions built for the 1929 exhibition. The more interesting is the Archaeological Museum, a neo-Renaissance building in which the exhibits include the Treasure of the Carambolo – a collection of jewellery from the semi-mythical civilisation of Tartessos, which existed in Andalucia in the 8th–9th centuries BC.

The other museum, the Museo de Artes y Costumbres Populares, houses a collection of folk arts and crafts. **Museo Arqueológico** ⓣ (954) 23 24 01 ⓦ www.juntadeandalucia.es/cultura); **Museo de Artes y Costumbres Populares** ⓣ (954) 23 25 76 ⓛ For both museums 14.30–20.30 Tues, 09.00–20.30 Wed–Sat, 09.00–14.30 Sun, closed Mon ⓘ Free to EU citizens

Museo de Bellas Artes

Seville's Museum of Fine Arts is claimed to be the second most important art gallery in Spain after the Prado in Madrid. It is housed in a 17th-century convent and has two floors arranged around three cloisters, all linked by a grand staircase. The building is appropriate since many of the works originally hung in convents and churches and are on religious themes. Although the museum has some sculpture and pieces of ceramics, jewellery and furniture (with exhibits dating from the Gothic period to the present day), the focus is on Seville's homegrown school of painting.

The core of the collection is from three masters of Sevillian baroque: Zurbarán, Murillo and Valdés Leal. ⓐ Pl. del Museo 9

▲ *The Museo de Bellas Artes houses one of Spain's most important art collections*

CARMEN

It's almost impossible to think of Seville's bullring without also thinking of Carmen, the tragic heroine of Bizet's opera of the same name. The story is based on an 1845 novella by Prosper Mérimée, who was inspired by a true story he heard from a countess while he was travelling in Spain. The eponymous Carmen is a strong-willed, mesmerising, manipulative young siren who attracts the attentions of a soldier, Don José, who is so besotted with her that he abandons his regiment. Carmen, however, spurns him in favour of a virile bullfighter, Escamillo. In a jealous rage, Don José springs on Carmen outside the bullring's Puerta del Principe and kills her as the crowds cheer Escamillo performing in the ring. The opera has proved to have an enduring appeal because it avoids easy moralising and Carmen, for all her faults, is likeable for her passion and her acceptance of her fate.

🕿 (954) 22 07 90 🅦 www.juntadeandalucia.es/cultura/museos/MBASE 🕔 14.30–20.30 Tues, 09.00–20.30 Wed–Sat, 09.00–14.30 Sun, closed Mon ❶ Free to EU citizens

RETAIL THERAPY

Antonio Bernal Get yourself a Spanish guitar made to order in this guitar builder's workshop across the road from Nervión Plaza. ⓐ Hernando del Pulgar 20 🕿 (954) 58 26 79 🅦 www.antoniobernal.com 🕔 10.00–14.00, 17.00–20.30 Mon–Fri, 10.00–14.00 Sat, closed Sun

Farrutx Mallorcan designer Farrutx creates classic, sexy shoes for women (with a smaller line for men). ⓐ Rioja 13 ❶ (954) 22 22 09 ⓦ www.farrutx.com ⓛ 10.00–13.30, 17.00–20.30 Mon–Fri, 10.00–12.00, 17.30–20.30 Sat, closed Sun

Nervión Plaza Shopping centre between Santa Justa station and the football stadium. To get there on foot follow the remains of the Roman aqueduct along Calle Luis Montoto. ⓐ Av. Luis Morales ❶ (954) 98 91 31 ⓦ www.nervionplaza.com ⓛ Shops 10.00–22.00, Restaurants 10.00–03.00

Pedro Algaba Galdón A bullfighter's tailor: suits of light for hire or sale, but good ones don't come cheap. It takes a month and a team of 40 people to make a full suit. If you just want a souvenir, there are swords, capes, hats, sticks, banderillas, symbols, handkerchiefs, keyrings and posters. ⓐ Adriano 39 in El Arenal, next to the Maestranza bullring ❶ (954) 27 78 72 ⓛ 10.15–14.00, 17.15–20.30 Mon–Fri, 10.15–14.00 Sat, closed Sun

Plaza de Armas A shopping and entertainment centre occupying the graceful engine shed of the former Córdoba railway station. ⓐ Pl. de la Legión ❶ (954) 90 82 82 ⓛ 10.00–22.00 (entertainment venues stay open later)

Seville Football Club official shop If flamenco dresses, fans and shawls are not for you, you can always take home a sporting memento of Seville. ⓐ Av. Eduardo Dato, Estadio Ramón Sánchez Pizjuán ❶ (954) 54 30 30 ⓦ www.sevillafc.es ⓛ 10.00–21.00 Mon–Sat (also opens two hours before the game starts on match days), closed Sun

TAKING A BREAK

Alcoy 10 £ ❶ A lively bar with tasty modern tapas that's a real gastronomic treat in this otherwise quiet residential part of town. ⓐ Alcoy 10 ⓣ (954) 90 57 02 ⓛ 08.30–00.00 Tues–Sat, 08.30–16.00 Sun, closed Mon

Bodeguita Antonio Romero £ ❷ The renowned selection of authentic Andalucian specialities available on the tapas menu – including a variety of *montaditos* (toasted sandwiches) – means that this place is often quite crowded. ⓐ Gamazo 16 ⓣ (954) 21 05 85 ⓛ 12.00–01.00 Tues–Sun, closed Mon

La Fábrica de la Cerveza £ ❸ No queues; no waiting: in this microbrewery bar you serve the beer yourself at a tap installed at your table. To go with the homebrew you can order tapas or a full meal. ⓐ Centro Comercial Pl. de Armas ⓣ (954) 90 88 28 ⓦ www.lafabrica-cerveceros.com ⓛ 12.00–01.00

La Giganta £ ❹ What they call 'tapas' here are in fact full portions, so order conservatively. Try the wild mushrooms with Roquefort or beef with prunes. ⓐ Alhóndiga 6 ⓣ (954) 21 09 75 ⓛ 12.30–16.30, 20.00–00.00 Mon–Sat, 12.30–16.30 Sun

Las Piletas £ ❺ As it opens at 07.00, this is a useful place to have breakfast. Later, tapas take over. ⓐ Marques de Paradas 28 ⓣ (954) 22 04 04 ⓛ 07.30–00.00

El Rinconcillo £ ❻ Seville's oldest bar is also one of its most atmospheric. ⓐ Gerona 40 ⓣ (954) 22 31 83 ⓦ www.elrinconcillo.es ⓛ 13.00–01.00

Seville's tapas bars offer a wide variety of choice

Taberna Manzanilla £ ❼ This small bar has tables spread in the triangular square across the road from El Rinconcillo. It has a good menu of tapas and also rents out rooms if you are in need of somewhere to stay. ⓐ Pl. de Terceros 7 (Sol 17) ❶ (954) 22 45 93 ❶ 12.00–17.00, 20.00–00.00

AFTER DARK

RESTAURANTS

Asador Salas £ ❽ Meat, fish and shellfish grilled over a fire of smouldering holm oakwood. ⓐ Almansa 15 ❶ (954) 21 77 96 ❶ 14.00–17.00, 20.00–01.00

Porta Rossa £ ❾ An elegant but unpretentious Italian restaurant, with superb fresh pasta dishes and a cosy ambience. ⓐ Pastor y Landero 20 ❶ (954) 21 61 39 ❶ 14.00–15.45, 21.00–23.45 Tues–Sat, 14.00–15.45 Sun, closed Mon

LIVE MUSIC

Fun Club Seville's longest-running club begins the night with a concert and continues it as a bar. Eclectic agenda from ethnic to electro. ⓐ Alameda de Hercules 86 ❶ (650) 48 98 58 ⓦ www.salafunclub.com ❶ Concerts 21.30, Club 00.00–07.00 Thur–Sat, 20.00–01.00 Sun, closed Mon–Wed

Naima Café Jazz A small and friendly jazz bar, with live acts on Saturdays and jam sessions on Sundays. ⓐ Trajano 47 ❶ (954) 38 24 85 ⓦ www.naimacafejazz.com ❶ 15.00–03.00

Terraza Capote A great place to be on a spring or summer evening. On Tuesdays you can enjoy flamenco with your cocktail and on Wednesdays it's theatre. Thursdays are given over to live Latin music. ⓐ Marqués de Contadero, next to Puente de Triana (Puente Isabel II) ⓣ (954) 56 38 58 or (680) 18 22 25 ⓛ 13.00–03.00 Apr–Oct, closed Nov–Mar

FLAMENCO SHOWS

El Arenal Having been in business since 1950, this is one of Seville's longest-running flamenco venues. ⓐ Rodo 7, between Arco del Postigo and the bullring ⓣ (954) 21 64 92 ⓦ www.tablaoarenal.com ⓛ Shows at 20.30 & 22.30

Casa Carmen For those looking for flamenco variety. ⓐ Marqués de Paradas ⓣ (954) 21 28 89 ⓦ www.casacarmenarteflamenco.com ⓛ 20.30–23.00 daily, one-hour show starts at 21.30

CLUBS

Bauhaus Café Serves up electro-house, tech-house and nu-lounge. ⓐ Marqués de Paradas 53 ⓣ (954) 22 42 10 ⓦ www.bauhauscafe.com ⓛ 12.00–03.00 Sun–Wed, 12.00–05.00 Thur–Sat

Buddha del Mar Chill out, funk, house, Latin, Spanish and international pop in the former railway station that is now the Plaza de Armas shopping centre. The restaurant serves Japanese, Thai and Chinese food. ⓐ Centro Comercial Plaza de Armas, Plaza de la Legion ⓣ (954) 08 90 95 ⓦ www.buddhadelmar.com ⓛ 15.30–03.00 Sun–Thur, 15.30–06.00 Fri & Sat. Admission charge Sat night

The river & beyond

Across the Guadalquivir from the city centre the city continues as a built-up island between two branches of the river. Step off the Puente de Isabel II, built of iron in 1852, and you'll find yourself in Triana, renowned as one of the cradles of flamenco and the source of all the beautiful ceramics to be seen in Seville. There are few sights as such but, if nothing else, you'll get some great views over the river.

To the south, Triana merges into the Barrio de los Remedios – nudging up to the site of the April Fair – which you will probably only stray into if you are looking for a particular shop, restaurant or club.

To the north, meanwhile, is the Isla de la Cartuja, an elongated strip of land rehabilitated for the Expo 92 world fair (see page 15). Since that brief moment of glory, the Cartuja has been in search of a new vision to steer its future. Parts of the site have been 'repurposed' as an urban theme park and a technological business park, with offices and laboratories installed in some of expo's architecturally striking pavilions. But much of the Cartuja has a neglected feel with a disused cable car and Ariadne rocket now surrounded by fields of weeds – and not a shop, bar or restaurant in sight. In the middle of the Isla de la Cartuja stands an incongruous, schizophrenic monument: a monastery that was converted into a ceramics factory in the Industrial Revolution and now serves as a museum of contemporary art.

SIGHTS & ATTRACTIONS

Guadalquivir River & its bridges

The Guadalquivir River has formed the watery backbone of Seville since Roman times when merchant vessels sailed upstream to deposit one cargo and leave with another. Later, fleets rolled up laden with

The river & beyond

0   250 metres
0   250 yards

N

Rio Guadalquivir

Puerta Norte
Puente del Alamillo
Instalaciones de Remo
Cartuja '93
Isla Mágica
Lago de España
ISLA DE LA CARTUJA
Puente de la Barqueta
Torre de los Perdigones
DON FADRIQUE AVENIDA
Basílica de La Macarena
CALLE RESOLANA
Pabellónes Internacionales
Jardines del Guadalquivir
Convento de San Clemente
C DEL PERA
C DE LA FERIA
LA MACARENA
CALLE DE RELATOR
C DE SAN LUIS
AVE AMÉRICO VESPUCIO
Parque de la
CALLE DE SANTA CLARA
CALLE LUMBRERAS
C MATA
CALLE DE RELATOR
Meandro de San Jerónimo
Auditorio
Convento de Santa Clara
ALAMEDA DE HERCULES
CALLE DE LA FERIA
Iglesia de San Luis
Monasterio de Santa María de las Cuevas
CAMINO DE LOS DESCABRIMIENTOS
Cartuja
C Reparad
DEL GRAN PODER
CALLE DE SANTA ANA
CALLE DE JUAN RABADAN
Puerto de Indias
Cuartel del Carmen
Conv Sta M la Real
CALLE DE JESUS
C DEL AMOR DE DIOS
CALLE CASTELLAR
Palacio de Las Dueñas
CALLE
DE
BANOS
C DE SAN VICENTE
CENTRO
PL DE LA ENCARNACIÓN
PLAZA DE TERCEROS
PL PONCE DE LEON
Iglesia de San Pedro
Puerto Triana
CALLE DE ALFONSO XII
C M VILLA
C DE LARAÑA IMAGEN
PL PAD JER CORD
Museo de Bellas Artes
CALLE DE SAN ELOY
PL SAN PEDRO
PL CRISTO DE SURG
Convento de San Leandro
Plaza de Armas
CALLE MARQUES DE PARADAS
CALLE DE BAILEN
C O'DONNELL
Palacio de Lebrija
Iglesia de la Anunciacion
Casa de Pilatos
AVE DEL CRISTO DE LA EXPIRACIÓN
Iglesia de la Magdalena
CALLE RIOJA
CALLE VELAZQUEZ
Iglesia del Salvador
CORRAL DEL REY
Sta M de Jesús
Pte del Cachorro
C DE SAN PABLO
PL NUEVA
Ayuntamiento
Mon Rom
PL MERC
Jardines de Chapina
CALLE DE ARIONA
CALLE ZARAGOZA
EL ARENAL
Palacio Arzobispal
Iglesia Santa Cruz
CALLE TEJARES PINZON
CALLE DE CASTILLA
CALLE DE ADRIANO
PL CABILDO
Catedral y Giralda
PL V REYES
PAGES DEL CORRO
TRIANA
PTE DE ISABEL II
Plaza de Toros de la Real Maestranza
PL DEL TRIUNFO
SANTA CRUZ
PL DEL ALTOZANO
PASEO DE CRISTOBAL COLÓN
Palacio de Cultura
Archivo de Indias
Reales Alcázares
CALLE DE SAN JACINTO
Dársena
PASEO MARQUES DE CONTADERO
CALLE SANTANDER
Jardines de Murillo y jardines
Monumento a Colón
PAGES DEL CORRO GENOVA
CALLE DE LA ASUNCION
CALLE DEL BETIS
Torre del Oro Museo Maritimo
PUERTA DE JEREZ
C SAN FERNANDO
Jardines Catalina de Ribera
CALLE EVANGELISTA
PTE S TELMO
Hotel Alfonso XIII
PL DON JUAN DE AUSTRIA
FARMACEÚTICO E M HERRERA
PLAZA DE LA CUBA
Palacio de San Telmo
Universidad
PALOS DE LA FRONTERA
AVENIDA DE LA REPUBLICA ARGENTINA
PASEO DE LAS DELICIAS
AVE DE M LUISA
Plaza de España
CALLE SALADO
CALLE CONSTANCIA

POI
Cathedral
Information
Police Station
Airport
Railway Stn
Bus Station
Hospital

gold and silver from the New World. There is still a functioning port, but it is largely dedicated to servicing tourist cruise ships.

The best bank to stroll along is on the city-centre side of the river, from the Torre del Oro to beyond the Plaza de Armas shopping centre. If you aren't feeling energetic, sit and enjoy the view from one of the bars and restaurants on Calle del Betis on the Triana side.

An even better way to enjoy the river is to take a short cruise with Cruceros Torre del Oro (see page 55).

The river is crossed by nine bridges, six of which were built for Expo 92 (see page 15). The two most interesting are the Puente del Alamillo (designed by the artist Santiago Calatrava) and the Puente de la Barqueta (opposite Isla Mágica theme park, see opposite), the most visible reminder of the heady days of the Expo for most Sevillanos.

▲ *Take a cruise boat and see the city from the river*

Isla Mágica

One of the few theme parks in the world in an urban area, the Magic Island is built around the lake that was at the heart of Expo 92 (see page 15). It is loosely divided into eight zones and has over 40 rides, games, shows and other attractions – including a freefall tower, a 16th-century merry-go-round, various big dippers, a llama rodeo, rafting rivers and a '4 dimension' virtual reality experience. ❶ Information (902) 16 17 16, Reservations (902) 16 00 00 Ⓦ www.islamagica.es ◑ Varies, check website

Triana

When you have drunk your fill of pretty-pretty Santa Cruz and seen enough of the grand monuments of central Seville, you might want to wander across the bridge into the more down-to-earth district of La Triana, which looks across the river at the bullring and the Torre del Oro. There are few historic sights here, but Triana has had plenty of history. To begin with it still bears its Roman name (deriving from Trajana, after the Emperor Trajan who was born in nearby Italica). Later, less appealingly, Triana was an early home to the Spanish Inquisition as recalled by the name of one of its streets, Callejón de la Inquisición. Being a working-class, waterside neighbourhood, Triana has always been a rich recruiting ground for sailors and adventurers and supplied many shiphands bound for the Americas.

There are three good reasons for coming to modern Triana. First, even if you get no further than the end of the bridge, you will enjoy good views looking back at the city centre. Better still, take a seat at an outdoor table of one of the bars and restaurants along Calle del Betis, from which you can gaze at the Torre del Oro and the bullring and watch cruise ships come and go.

TRIANA CERAMICS

The first record of ceramics being produced in Triana dates from 1314, but it is widely accepted that the industry is much older than that. It is probable that the Romans produced amphorae here to transport oil and wine. In the Moorish period, Triana's potteries outside the city walls were busy producing the blue, white and green ceramic tiles, *azulejos*, that form such an essential part of interior decorations of buildings of the time. The characteristics of modern Triana pottery are considered to have been established by an Italian craftsman, Francisco Nicoloso Pisano, who settled in Triana at the end of the 15th century. In the 18th century, there was a great demand for painted tiles depicting religious images and realistic themes. Contemporary Triana ceramicists still make large mosaic scenes and signs for a variety of uses around the city.

Second, this is the place to buy ceramics. It is the source of all the murals to be seen around central Seville and there are still about 40 functioning shops, studios, factories and workshops, most of which are open to visitors. The oldest and most popular is Cerámica Santa Ana (see page 100).

The third lure is flamenco. This is Seville's traditional gypsy quarter and proudly claims to be one of the birthplaces of flamenco (an honour tacitly shared with Jerez de la Frontera). Although you can see highly organised, professional shows in Santa Cruz, a purist would argue that you need to stumble on an impromptu combination of singer,

◀ *Triana is the place to seek out authentic flamenco*

⬤ *The colourful façade of Cerámica Santa Ana*

guitarist and dancer swept up in the frenzy of spontaneous emotion in some uncelebrated Triana dive to understand what flamenco is really about.

CULTURE

Monasterio de Santa María de las Cuevas (Centro Andaluz de Arte Contemporáneo)

In 1248, according to tradition, a statue of the Virgin Mary was found in one of the caves north of Triana from which clay to feed the potteries was extracted. A monastery dedicated to 'Our Lady of the Caves' grew up on the site. Columbus stayed in it, and his family had close links with it after his death. A magnificent ombu tree in its grounds is said to have been planted by Hernando Columbus, the son of the explorer.

The monastery was abandoned in 1835. Soon after, the buildings were leased by Charles Pickman, a merchant from Liverpool, who built kilns and installed machinery to churn out ceramics to meet local demand. Production continued into the 1970s.

In 1992 the monastery-factory formed a centrepiece for the Expo (see page 15). Since then it has housed Andalucia's contemporary art gallery, but this institution is rather cowed by its setting. At the heart of the complex is a rather plain church with a pretty Mudéjar patio off it in which the pallid statues of two nuns kneel at prayer.

But it's more the factory features that impress. A line of iron-girdered chimneys physically overshadow the other buildings, and

ELCANO'S ROUND-THE-WORLD VOYAGE

It's usually Magellan who is credited in the record books with the first circumnavigation of the globe, but this isn't quite accurate. Although he set off from Seville in command of a mission to sail around the world, he didn't make it back to claim the honour. Tragically, he was killed in a battle in the Philippines. So it was left to one his crewmen, a Spanish Basque, Juan Sebastián Elcano (whom Magellan had previously chained up and condemned to death for mutiny) to lead the expedition back to its starting point. On 8 September 1522 Elcano, along with the remaining 19 sailors from the 200 who had set out three years before, sailed into Seville on the only surviving ship of the expedition, the *Victoria*. Magellan may get all the mentions in history books, but at least Elcano has a street named after him in Triana.

there are various reminders that functional art was once churned out here to earn workers and masters a living. One entrance porch is entirely covered with neat rows of ornamental tiles like a salesman's samples book left permanently open. And the entrance on the river side of the monastery (not the main entrance) is a rather cute tiled gateway.
ⓐ Av. Américo Vespucio 2 ⓣ (955) 03 70 70 ⓦ www.caac.es ⓛ Monastery and gallery 10.00–21.00 Tues–Fri, 11.00–20.00 Sat, 10.00–15.00 Sun, Apr–Sept; 10.00–20.00 Tues–Fri, 11.00–20.00 Sat, 10.00–15.00 Sun, Oct–Mar; closed Mon. Gallery free on Tues; grounds free

RETAIL THERAPY

Cerámica Santa Ana Triana's most famous ceramics factory, which has been going since 1870. Reproduction historical pieces are available.
ⓐ San Jorge 31 (off Pl. del Altozano) ⓣ (954) 33 39 90 ⓛ 09.30–14.00, 17.00–20.30 Mon–Sat, Sept–July; 09.20–14.00 Mon–Fri, 10.00–14.00 Sat, Aug, closed Sun

Tierra Nuestra Seville's first specialist wine shop, and still arguably the best. ⓐ Constancia 41 ⓣ (954) 28 46 82 ⓛ 10.00–14.00, 18.00–21.00 Mon–Sat, closed Sun

TAKING A BREAK

El Faro de Triana £ ❶ The Triana Lighthouse ought to be classed as one of the city's landmarks, being a yellow tower with clock turret stuck to the end of Puente de Isabel II. Squeeze through the small bar and up the stairs where there are two small terraces with tables offering unbeatable views over the river. ⓐ Puente de Isabel II (Puente de Triana) ⓣ (954) 33 61 92 ⓛ Bar 10.00–01.00, Restaurant 11.00–16.30, 19.30–00.30

⬥ *Puente de Isabel II with El Faro de Triana first on the left*

Sol y Sombra £ ❷ One of the authentic old bars of Andalucia, decorated with bullfighting posters and serving tapas such as prawns with ham and spicy sausages. ⓐ Castilla 147–151 ❶ (954) 33 39 35 ⓦ www.tabernasolysombra.com ❶ 13.00–16.00, 21.00–00.00

AFTER DARK

RESTAURANTS

San Marco ££ ❸ Exquisite cuisine – Spanish with some Italian influence – in an elegant 18th-century house on the side of Calle del Betis away from the riverbank. ⓐ Betis 68 ❶ (954) 28 03 10 ❶ 13.30–16.30, 20.30–00.30 Wed–Mon, closed Tues

Río Grande £££ ❹ Three restaurants share terraces with more or less the same view. This one, strong on fish and seafood, is immediately next to Puente San Telmo. Next to it is the Asador de Triana and a little further on the Kiosco de las Flores. ⓐ Betis 31A ⓣ (954) 27 39 56 ⓦ www.riogrande-sevilla.com ⓛ 13.00–16.00, 20.00–00.00

FLAMENCO SHOWS

Given its role in the history of flamenco, you would have thought Triana would be the best place to see the art form at its purest. And in one way that's true. The problem is tracking down authentic flamenco. All the most organised and well-advertised venues are back across the river in Santa Cruz and El Arenal. In Triana you have to keep your ears open and hope you stumble upon some bar where an impromptu performer has just acquired *el duende* – the indefinable spirit or passion that can't be bought or learned. Good bars to start your search for flamenco are:

El Ancla ⓐ Pagés del Corro 43 ⓣ (954) 34 09 56 ⓛ 21.00–02.00 Tues–Sat, closed Sun & Mon

Casa Anselma ⓐ Pagés del Corro 49 ⓛ 20.00–02.00 Tues–Sun, closed Mon, July & Aug

La Madrugá ⓐ Salado 11 ⓣ (657) 97 06 10 ⓦ www.madrugasevilla.com ⓛ 23.00–02.00

CLUBS

Al Alba A starkly designed bar, somewhat characterless in the early evening, which later becomes what is probably the only flamenco disco in town. ⓐ Betis 41 ⓦ www.alalbasevilla.com ⓛ 18.30–03.30

Discoteca Boss A discotheque on the banks of the Guadalquivir with a variety of levels and spaces at your disposal. ⓐ Betis 67 ⓣ (954) 99 01 04 ⓦ www.salaboss.es ⓛ 00.00–06.00 Wed–Sun, closed Tues

▶ *The lovely Andalucian 'white town' of Olvera*

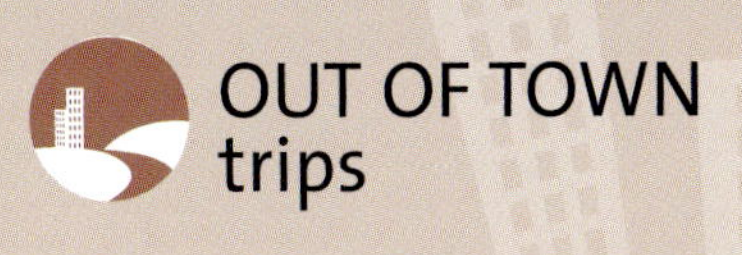

Days out from Seville

There are several places easily reached from Seville. Closest of them are the Roman ruins of Itálica (see page 109). Another rewarding short day trip is to the equally historic (but living) town of Carmona (see page 106). For fresh air and wildlife, meanwhile, you need to head straight for the outstanding Doñana National Park (see page 108). An hour to the south is the province of Cádiz and the city of Jerez de la Frontera (see page 110), famous for its sherries, dancing horses and flamenco music.

GETTING THERE

Driving yourself or enjoying the scenery by bus are easily the best options for getting to these areas from Seville, although trains do run to Jerez de la Frontera. Whichever option you choose, you'll be there within an hour.

By rail

There are frequent trains between Jerez de la Frontera and Seville, leaving from the city's Santa Justa Station (see page 48).

By road

Lots of buses run every day to Carmona and Santiponce (in Itálica) from Plaza de Armas (see page 49). If you prefer to drive from Seville: for Itálica, take the N630 north; for Carmona, take the N4 northeast; for Doñana National Park, go south from the west-bound A49; and for Jerez de la Frontera, take the N4 south.

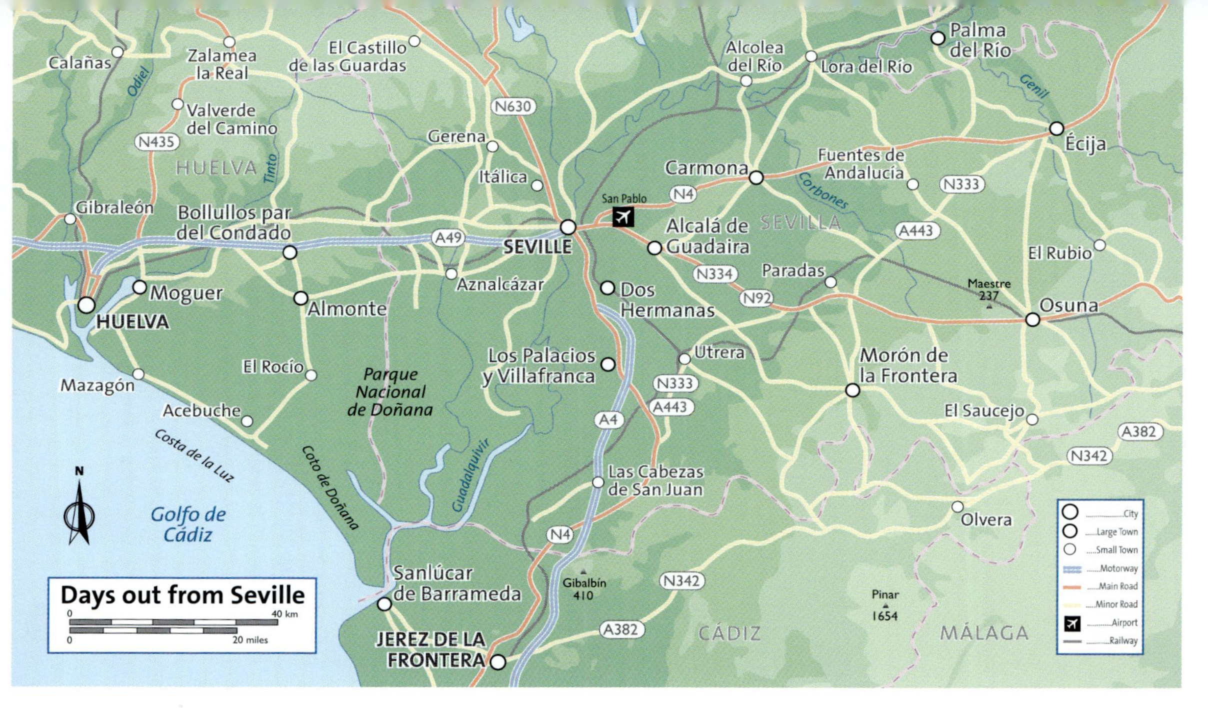

Calañas
Odiel
Zalamea la Real
El Castillo de las Guardas
Alcolea del Río
Lora del Río
Palma del Río
Genil
Valverde del Camino
N435
N630
HUELVA
Tinto
Gerena
Itálica
Carmona
Fuentes de Andalucía
Corbones
N333
Écija
Gibraleón
Bollullos par del Condado
San Pablo
N4
Alcalá de Guadaira
SEVILLA
A443
El Rubio
A49
SEVILLE
N334
Paradas
Maestre 237
Moguer
Aznalcázar
Dos Hermanas
N92
Osuna
HUELVA
Almonte
Utrera
Morón de la Frontera
El Rocío
Los Palacios y Villafranca
N333
Mazagón
Parque Nacional de Doñana
A443
El Saucejo
Acebuche
A4
A382
Costa de la Luz
Guadalquivir
N342
Coto de Doñana
Las Cabezas de San Juan
N
Golfo de Cádiz
N4
Olvera
Gibalbín 410
N342
Sanlúcar de Barrameda
Pinar 1654
Days out from Seville
0   40 km
0   20 miles
JEREZ DE LA FRONTERA
A382
CÁDIZ
MÁLAGA

City
Large Town
Small Town
Motorway
Main Road
Minor Road
Airport
Railway

SIGHTS & ATTRACTIONS

Carmona

The historic town of Carmona, sitting on an outcrop of rock looking over plains, is an easy day trip or even half-day up the motorway from Seville. Both the Romans and the Moors have left an indelible mark on it.

From the Moorish arch of the Puerta de Sevilla (home of the tourist information office) – which lets you through what's left of the ramparts – narrow streets climb up to the main square, the Plaza San Fernando, which is lined with some fine 17th- and 18th-century houses. The upper storeys of one corner house are photogenically faced in blue tiles.

Continue in the same direction and you'll come to the Gothic Iglesia de Santa María (on Plaza del Marqués de las Torres), which retains the ablutionary patio of the former mosque and also has a Visigothic calendar. Next to it is the **Museo de la Ciudad** (ⓐ Palacio Marqués de las Torres, San Ildefonso 1 ⓣ (954) 14 01 28 ⓦ www.museociudad.carmona.org) telling the story of Carmona from the Stone Age to the present day.

Further on, the town comes to an abrupt halt at another gateway, the Puerta de Córdoba, with its two octagonal towers. Beyond, the land drops steeply away. Retrace your steps and follow the signs to the parador, one of the state-run chain of hotels that often occupy historic buildings. This one is in the former fortress-palace of King Pedro I, which overhangs the cliff giving an unbroken view of the vast plain of sunflowers and cereals below where, in 206 BC, Scipio defeated Hasrubal the Carthaginian in battle.

Outside the old town are two more Roman sites of interest: an amphitheatre (closed to the public, but you can see it from outside)

The Moorish Puerta de Sevilla at Carmona

and the Roman necropolis, the **Necropolis Romana** (ⓐ Av. Jorge Bónsor 95 ⓣ (955) 62 46 15 ⓦ www.carmona.org). Around 250 of the 800 family tombs that lie on the hillside in between the cypress trees have been excavated and put on display. The largest have vestibules and one, the Servilia Tomb, is as big as a small villa. The so-called Elephant Tomb, meanwhile, has benches for funeral banquets and what's thought to have been a kitchen.

Tourist information ⓐ Alcázar de la Puerta de Sevilla ⓣ (954) 19 09 55 ⓦ www.turismo.carmona.org ⓛ 10.00–18.00 Mon–Sat, 10.00–15.00 Sun

PARQUE NACIONAL DE DOÑANA (DOÑANA NATIONAL PARK)

The marshes, woods and sand dunes at the mouth of the Guadalquivir River make up one of Europe's largest and most important national parks.

Access is strictly controlled to protect the wildlife (most spectacularly the lynx and imperial eagle) that clings on in this fragile habitat, but Doñana's policy is one of controlling tourism rather than excluding it altogether.

There are five visitors' centres on the fringes of the park, the one at Aznalcázar being the closest to Seville. Probably the best one to head for, though, is Acebuche, which can be reached via El Rocío (a town that is dead most of the year but springs to life for a big Whitsuntide pilgrimage – see Annual events, page 9).

All the visitors' centres give out information and have displays about the flora and fauna in the park. But the only way to appreciate Doñana properly is to take a guided tour in a camouflaged bus. The trip takes four hours and covers 70 km

(43 miles), taking in a representative sample of all the major ecosystems of the park. An alternative way to see a little of Doñana is to take a boat trip from the Fabrica de Hielo visitors' centre at Bajo de Guía just outside Sanlúcar de Barrameda.

Of course, the wildlife you see depends on the time of year, the weather and luck. Most of the mammals in the park are difficult to spot and inevitably a lot of the interest is in the bird life. Doñana's marshes are on one of the main migration routes, and autumn and spring can be good times for birdwatching.

Aznalcázar Information Point ❶ (955) 75 02 09
Acebuche Visitors' Centre ❶ (959) 43 04 32
Ⓦ www.donanavisitas.com
Guided tours ⓐ Trips depart from Acebuche Visitors' Centre ❶ 08.30 & 17.00 Mon–Sat, June–mid-Sept; 08.30 & 15.00 Tues–Sun, mid-Sept–May ❶ Booking essential
Boat trips ⓐ Depart from Bajo de Guía, Sanlúcar de Barrameda ❶ (956) 36 38 13 Ⓦ www.visitasdonana.com ❶ 10.00 Nov–Feb; 10.00 & 16.00 Mar–May & Oct; 10.00 & 17.00 June–Sept ❶ Booking essential

Itálica

Although Seville was founded by the Romans, it is long predated by its now insignificant neighbour, Itálica, at Santiponce just beyond the northern outskirts. This municipality was founded by Scipio Africanus in 206 BC to settle veteran soldiers of the Second Punic War. It was later the birthplace of the Emperor Trajan (born in AD 53), who ruled over the empire when it was at its maximum extent.

However, Itálica still hadn't reached the peak of its importance, which came in the 2nd century AD. Then, like the rest of the Roman Empire, it fell to the barbarian invasions of the 5th century. It was further ravaged in the 8th century by the Moors and its ruins subsequently plundered for building materials, which were incorporated into the fabric of Seville. Its ruined streets and monuments are still impressive as ruins go – especially a round mosaic floor and the elliptical amphitheatre in which 25,000 spectators could cram to watch gladiatorial contests. The most interesting finds, though, are now in museums in Seville (and some of them in Madrid).

Information Centre ⓐ Av. de Extemadura 2, Santiponce ❶ (955) 99 73 76 Ⓦ www.ayto-santiponce.es

Jerez de la Frontera

It may not sound like it, but this city gave its name to the world's most popular aperitif, sherry. In fact, *bodegas* producing fortified wines make up one half of Jerez's tourist appeal, and dancing horses make up the rest.

The **Fundación Real Escuela Andaluza de Arte Ecuestre** (Royal Horse School ⓐ Av. Duque de Abrantes ❶ (956) 31 80 08 or 31 96 35 Ⓦ www.realescuela.org) has got tourist management down to a fine art and if you like horses you shouldn't come away disappointed. You can take the full tour, which includes watching training sessions and visiting the stables, the tack room, the saddlery, the palace rooms, the Museum of Equestrian Arts and the Carriage Museum. Alternatively, if you are short of time or interest, you can opt for the slightly cheaper 'half visit'.

Better, though, is to see a show of the school's highly trained white steeds performing ballet routines. Best of all is to be here in May for Jerez's Feria del Caballo (Horse Fair) with its parades and

🔺 *Jerez cathedral from a shady side street*

○ *Take a tour of the Bodega González Byass at Jerez*

dancing by both humans and animals. The soundtrack to this and other fiestas is flamenco music, of which Jerez claims to be one of the authentic cradles (along with Seville).

As for sherry, you could fill a couple of days finding out about and tasting the stuff, but if you are just curious, visit one of the big *bodegas* such as **González Byass** – home of Tío Pepe, supposedly Spain's best-known brand abroad – (ⓐ Manuel María González 12 ① (956) 35 70 00 Ⓦ www.gonzalezbyass.es Ⓛ Guided tours in English 11.30, 12.30, 13.30, 15.30, 16.30 & 17.30 Sept–June; 11.30, 12.30, 13.30, 16.30, 17.30 & 18.30 Jul & Aug) or **Domecq** (ⓐ San Ildefonso 3 ① (956) 15 15 00 Ⓦ www.domecqbodegas.com Ⓛ Tours at 11.00, 12.00 & 13.00 Mon & Wed, 11.00, 12.00, 13.00 & 14.00 Tues, Thur & Fri, 12.00 & 14.00 Sat). **Tourist information** ⓐ Alameda Cristina, Edificio los Claustros ① (956) 34 17 11 or 33 88 74 Ⓦ www.turismojerez.com

RETAIL THERAPY

La Casa del Jerez Sells souvenirs of Jerez and gives you the opportunity to taste wines before you buy. ⓐ Urbanización Divina Pastora Local 3 (opposite the Real Escuela Andaluza del Arte Ecuestre) ❶ (956) 33 51 84 ❷ 10.00–15.00, 18.00–21.00 Mon–Fri, 10.00–15.00 Sat, closed Sun

TAKING A BREAK

Carmona

Mesón Sierra Mayor £–££ This atmospheric bar-restaurant specialising in cured hams occupies the old stables of the same historic mansion which contains Carmona's museum. Even if you are not female, ask for the key to the ladies' toilet to see an ingenious bit of antique plumbing. ⓐ San Ildefonso 1, Palacio Marqués de las Torres (Museo de la Ciudad) ❶ (954) 14 44 04 ❷ 12.00–23.00 Mon–Sat, closed Sun

La Alacena de Carmona ££ A friendly new tapas bar serving tasty modern tapas and various wines by the glass. ⓐ Pl. de Lasso 2 ❶ (954) 19 62 00 ❷ 12.00–23.00 Mon–Fri, 11.00–00.00 Sat, closed Sun

La Yedra ££ A restaurant in a pleasing courtyard near the parador. ⓐ General Freire 8 ❶ (954) 14 45 25 ❷ 13.00–16.15, 20.30–23.15 Tues–Sat, 13.00–16.15 Sun, closed Mon

Jerez de la Frontera

El Gallo Azul £ A semicircular bar with dining room above commanding a view of the street life of Jerez, such as it is (it vanishes when the shops close). Domecq wines served along with hot, tasty, varied tapas.

ⓐ Larga 2 ⓣ (956) 32 61 48 ⓛ Bar 11.00–00.00 Mon–Sat, Restaurant 13.00–16.00, 20.00–23.15 Mon–Sat, closed Sun

Juanito ££ An old bar famous for serving the best tapas in town. ⓐ Pescadería Vieja 8–10 ⓣ (956) 33 48 38 ⓛ 13.00–17.00, 20.30–23.00

Sanlúcar de Barrameda

Mirador de Doñana ££ One of a number of waterside restaurants with a view across the beach and river to the national park. Fish and seafood on the menu. ⓐ Bajo de Guia, Sanlúcar de Barrameda ⓣ (956) 36 42 05 ⓛ 13.15–16.30, 20.15–00.00 Mon–Sat, closed Sun

AFTER DARK

Jerez de la Frontera

La Taberna Flamenca £ A flamenco restaurant housed in a former *bodega*. Usefully for anyone who doesn't like late nights, the show is at 14.30 most days (check times when you reserve), while you digest your lunch. It lasts about 50 minutes. ⓐ Angostillo de Santiago 3, in front of Iglesia de Santiago ⓣ (956) 32 36 93 ⓦ www.latabernaflamenca.com ⓛ Restaurant 13.30–16.00, 20.00–00.00 June–Oct, 13.30–16.00, 20.00–00.00 Tues–Sat, closed Sun & Mon Nov–May

ACCOMMODATION

Carmona

El Rincón de las Descalzas ££–£££ A small, homely hotel around three flowery patios in which the peace is only disturbed by the sound of classical music and a trickling fountain. ⓐ Descalzas 1 ⓣ (954) 19 11 72 ⓦ www.elrincondelasdescalzas.com

Casa de Carmona £££ A luxurious hotel that unashamedly offers
a taste of 'the lifestyle of the authentic Spanish nobility'. ⓐ Pl. de
Lasso 1 ⓣ (954) 19 10 00 ⓦ www.casadecarmona.com

Parador de Carmona £££ The principal monument of Carmona,
its 14th-century castle, is also its finest hotel with a tremendous
view over the plains. At the foot of the cliff is the parador's enticing
swimming pool. ⓐ Alcázar del Rey Don Pedro ⓣ (954) 14 10 10
ⓦ www.parador.es

Jerez de la Frontera
Bellas Artes ££ An old stone house restored using authentic
materials. Individually styled rooms. Private car park for guests.
ⓐ Pl. del Arroyo 45 ⓣ (956) 34 84 30 ⓦ www.hotelbellasartes.com

Palacio Garvey ££–£££ Restored 1850 neoclassical mansion in the
old part of Jerez. Small swimming pool. No time limit for breakfast.
Access for guests with disabilities. ⓐ Pl. Rafael Rivero, Tornería 24
ⓣ (956) 32 67 00 ⓦ www.sferahoteles.net

El Rocío
Hotel La Malvasia ££ An unexpected find in sleepy, remote El Rocío,
this is a sumptuously designed boutique hotel, with a great restaurant,
for very reasonable rates. ⓐ Sanlúcar 38 ⓣ (959) 44 38 70
ⓦ www.lamalvasiahotel.com

Sanlúcar de Barrameda
Los Helechos £ A friendly, bright, white, plant-filled hotel in the town
from which the Doñana boat excursions depart. ⓐ Madre de Dios 9
ⓣ (956) 36 76 55 ⓦ www.hotelloshelechos.com

The white towns

Brilliantly whitewashed hill towns and villages, often occupying dramatic sites and laid out higgledy-piggledy across the contours, are emblematic of Andalucia. The most picturesque of *los pueblos blancos* are concentrated in the sierras of Cádiz province, southeast of Seville, within the range of an overnight trip from the city. Several of these towns are still looked down upon by indomitable medieval fortresses, and their narrow, shady streets have changed little over the centuries. The countryside is often ruggedly spectacular, and the mountains make excellent territory for hiking, biking and nature-watching. This corner of Spain is strikingly green and wooded, and the air smells clean. Much of this route is within the **Parque Natural Sierra de Grazalema** nature reserve (ⓐ Av. de la Diputación, El Bosque ❶ (956) 71 60 63).

GETTING THERE

By road

You'll need a car to explore properly: take the N4 motorway south towards Jerez de la Frontera, then turn onto the main road to Arcos de la Frontera. Here a side road branches off for El Bosque and Grazalema. A scenic road climbs over the pass between Grazalema to Zahara de la Sierra. From there you can pick up the main road again for Ronda. As these towns and villages, with their tapering alleys, steps and dead ends at every turn, were built long before cars were ever thought of, it's best to park outside and walk in.

There are daily buses to Ronda from Plaza de Armas.

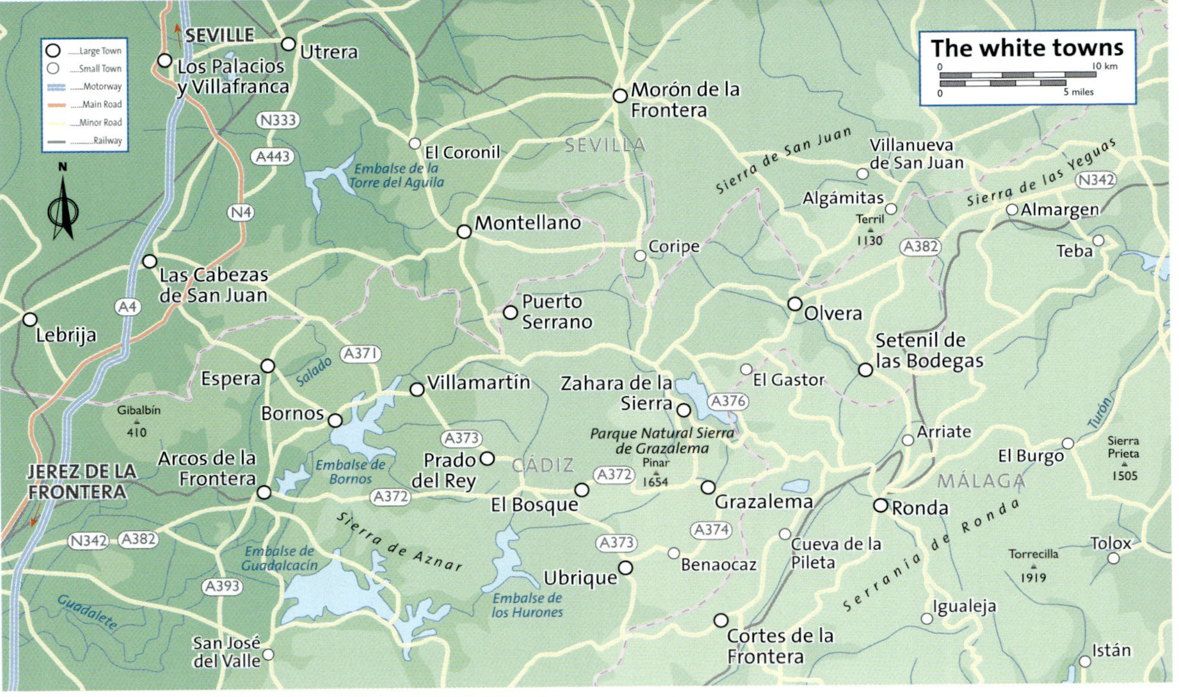

The white towns
0 10 km
0 5 miles
Large Town
Small Town
Motorway
Main Road
Minor Road
Railway
N
SEVILLE
Utrera
Los Palacios y Villafranca
N333
A443
N4
A4
Lebrija
Las Cabezas de San Juan
El Coronil
Embalse de la Torre del Aguila
Morón de la Frontera
SEVILLA
Montellano
Coripe
Sierra de San Juan
Villanueva de San Juan
Algámitas
Terril 1130
A382
Sierra de las Yeguas
N342
Almargen
Teba
Puerto Serrano
Olvera
Setenil de las Bodegas
Espera
Salado
A371
Villamartín
Zahara de la Sierra
A376
El Gastor
Gibalbín 410
Bornos
A373
Prado del Rey
CÁDIZ
Parque Natural Sierra de Grazalema
Pinar 1654
A372
Arriate
El Burgo
Sierra Prieta 1505
Turón
Arcos de la Frontera
Embalse de Bornos
A372
El Bosque
Grazalema
A374
Ronda
MÁLAGA
JEREZ DE LA FRONTERA
N342
A382
Embalse de Guadalcacín
Sierra de Aznar
A373
Benaocaz
Cueva de la Pileta
Serranía de Ronda
Torrecilla 1919
Tolox
A393
Guadalete
Embalse de los Hurones
Ubrique
San José del Valle
Cortes de la Frontera
Igualeja
Istán

SIGHTS & ATTRACTIONS

Arcos de la Frontera

The point of access to the white towns from Seville is Arcos de la Frontera, which, despite the expanding modern estates of houses around its fringes, has an unchanging old heart at the top of the town where the buildings creep right up to the lip of a breathtaking precipice.

The best way to get here is to drive. Park in the Plaza de España if you are travelling by car and walk up Calle Corredera to the main square of the old part of town, the Plaza del Cabildo. This is overlooked by the church of Santa Maria de la Asuncion, whose Plateresque west façade takes on a golden glow in the afternoon sun. To one side of the square a balcony provides views over the countryside below. Most of Arcos' shops, bars, hotels and restaurants are in the narrow streets around the Plaza del Cabildo.

Tourist information ⓐ Pl. del Cabildo ⓣ (956) 70 22 64
ⓦ www.arcosdelafrontera.es ⓛ 10.00–14.30, 16.00–19.00 Mon–Fri, 10.30–13.30, 16.00–18.00 Sat, 10.30–13.30 Sun

Grazalema

It may well be raining when you visit Grazalema because this is the place with the highest rainfall in Spain (by quantity of water falling, not number of wet days). That said, at least it keeps the surrounding countryside green.

Overlooked by crags of limestone, the town is used as a base by visitors to the nearby nature reserve of the same name, which is good for birdwatching, botanising or just walking around. The town itself has a small traditional weaving industry making blankets (see page 124).

From Grazalema (best reached by car), a scenic road climbs over Las Palomas Pass (1,357 m/4,452 ft) giving stunning views. On the

⬤ *The old town at Arcos de la Frontera*

way up you go through forests that harbour a rare species of tree, the Spanish fir (*Abies pinsapo*). It grows only in four locations over 1,000 m (3,281 ft) and they are kept under guard. Above the cliffs you are likely to see vultures soaring overhead.

CUEVA DE LA PILETA

This extensive cave contains some of the best and most curious prehistoric art in Europe: symbols in yellow and red; 360 feathery characters that may be some kind of writing (although the language may never be deciphered); and representations of animals, including a large fish. The paintings here were created at the same time as, or perhaps even earlier than, the more famous ones at Altamira in northern Spain. However, their significance, as with all prehistoric art, remains a matter of conjecture.

Interestingly, the cave was only found in 1905, by a local farmer who was hunting for bat droppings; it was not until six years later that a British ornithologist, Colonel Willoughby Verner, identified it as prehistoric.

Visits are by guided tour only, lasting around an hour. Numbers are limited, but it is possible to reserve a place by phone only on the first tour of the day. ⓐ Four km (just over two miles) from Benaoján off the MA501 towards Cortes de la Frontera ⓣ (952) 16 73 43 ⓦ www.cuevadelapileta.org ⓛ Tours 10.00–13.00 (leaving when there are sufficient people), 16.00 & 17.00

Tourist information ⓐ Pl. de España 11 ⓣ (956) 13 20 73 ⓛ 10.00–14.00, 16.00–20.00 Mon–Fri, 10.00–20.00 Sat & Sun, Nov–Apr; 10.00–14.00, 16.00–21.00 Mon–Fri, 10.00–21.00 Sat & Sun, May–Oct

Ronda

It's hard to imagine a more dramatic site for a town than on the edge of a cliff and astride a gorge. Ronda is justly the most famous of the

● *A cortijo, or farmhouse, near Arcos*

white towns and also the most touristy because of its proximity to the Costa del Sol.

The town is literally cut in two by a 90-m-deep (295-ft) gorge (El Tajo) of the River Guadalevín. Puente Nuevo (New Bridge), a feat of 18th-century engineering, crosses it. Its central section was once used as a prison. To get the best view of it, take the path down into the gorge from Plaza del Campillo (at the end of Calle Tenorio) or drive down Camino de los Molinos (from the Almocabar Gate) and climb up to the Arabic Arch. A visitors' centre explains the history of the bridge with an audiovisual presentation.

The next most popular sight in Ronda is the bullring, the **Plaza de Toros** (ⓐ Virgen de la Paz 15 ⓣ (952) 87 41 32), which is the oldest

The incredible El Tajo gorge at Ronda

in Spain and contains a bullfighting museum. The standard, modern form of bullfighting – on foot rather than on horseback – originated in Ronda in the 18th century, and this is commemorated by a 'Goya-esque' bullfight in period dress in September. Ronda has produced two famous 'dynasties' of bullfighters, the Romeros and the Ordóñezs. Arguably the most successful bullfighter ever was Pedro Romero,

who retired in 1799 remarking: 'Bearing in mind the 28 years that
I have been killing bulls, on average 200 bulls a year, I reckon that
I have killed approximately 5,600 bulls, if not more.' And all without
suffering a single scratch. Attached to the bullring is a museum
of bullfighting, the **Museo Taurino** (ⓐ Paseo Cristóbal Colón 12
ⓣ (954) 22 45 37 ⓛ 10.00–13.00 Mon–Fri, closed Sat & Sun).

The town has half a dozen other museums, of which the most
interesting is the **Museo del Bandolero** (ⓐ Armiñan 65 ⓣ (952) 87 77 85
ⓦ www.museobandolero.com), whose theme is banditry in the
surrounding mountains.

One other essential sight is the best-preserved suite of Moorish
baths (Baños Árabes) in Spain, which have brick horseshoe arches
holding up barrel vaults pierced with star-shaped skylights.
Tourist information ⓐ Paseo de Blas Infante ⓣ (952) 18 71 19
ⓦ www.turismoderonda.es ⓛ 09.30–19.30 Mon–Fri, 10.00–14.00,
15.30–18.30 Sat & Sun

Setenil de las Bodegas

Setenil is an atypical white town because of its site. Rather than
being high up on a crag or hillside it winds through a gorge, using
the rock overhangs as roofs for some of its houses and transforming
one street into a tunnel. In the middle of it is a 16th-century church
on a rock next to an Arab tower, from the battlements of which you
can get a view of the town.
Tourist information ⓐ Villa 2 ⓣ (956) 13 42 61 ⓦ www.setenil.com
ⓛ 10.30–14.00, 16.00–19.00 Tues–Sun, closed Mon

Zahara de la Sierra

A compact zigzag cluster of white houses at the base of a rock
crowned by a castle, Zahara has a strong claim to be the prettiest of

the white towns. There are not many streets, but they are pleasant to stroll around. Naturally, there are great views from the castle if you can face a stiff 10–15-minute walk. At Corpus Christi (May or June) the streets of Zahara are decorated with an impressive mass of greenery brought in from the surrounding countryside.

RETAIL THERAPY

Artesanía Textil de Grazalema Maintains the traditional woollen industry. Its small factory, in which blankets and ponchos are woven from local wool using hand-operated looms, is open to the public. Products are on sale in a shop on the premises. ⓐ Carretera de Ubrique-Ronda, Grazalema ⓣ (956) 13 20 08 ⓦ www.mantasdegrazalema.com ⓛ 08.00–14.00, 15.00–18.30 Mon–Thur, morning only on Fri, closed Sat & Sun

TAKING A BREAK

Arcos de la Frontera
El Convento £ A restaurant in a 17th-century palace with a small hotel in an adjacent building. ⓐ Marqués de Torresoto 7 ⓣ (956) 70 32 22 ⓛ 13.00–16.00, 19.00–22.00 Mon–Sat, Mar–Oct, closed Sun & Nov–Feb

Mesón el Patio £ An efficient, family-run restaurant in the old part of town serving traditional home-made food. There's a choice of four set menus all at the same very reasonable price. There's also a *pensión* in which some of the rooms have terraces with views. ⓐ Callejón de las Monjas 4 ⓣ (956) 70 23 02 ⓛ 12.00–17.00, 19.30–23.00 Thur–Tues, closed Wed

Ronda

La Giralda £ A bar that's a Ronda institution for its varied tapas. ⓐ Nueva 19
ⓣ (952) 87 28 02 ⓛ 12.00–16.30, 20.00–00.00 Thur–Tues, closed Wed

El Portón £ Popular bar for its home cooking, the speciality being
bull's tail. ⓐ Pedro Romero 7 ⓣ (952) 87 74 20 ⓛ 12.00–16.00,
19.30–23.00 Mon–Sat, closed Sun

Almocábar ££ In the residential Barrio de San Francisco at the
south end of town is this superb tapas bar and restaurant, where
the speciality is beef served sizzling on a tablet of hot volcanic
stone. ⓐ Pl. Ruedo Alameda 5 ⓣ (952) 87 59 77 ⓛ 13.30–16.30,
20.30–00.00 Mon, Wed–Sun, closed Tues

Restaurante Moreno ££ A Ronda classic, though a little hard to find
(it's near the railway station). There's no menu but a great meal of
fresh seafood or grilled steak is assured, no matter how limited your
Spanish. ⓐ Av. Ricardo Naverrete 4 ⓣ (952) 87 58 88 ⓛ 12.30–16.30,
20.00–00.00 Mon, Thur–Sun, 12.30–16.30 Tues, closed Wed

Setenil de las Bodegas

Las Flores £ A village bar-restaurant serving straightforward but
wholesome food. ⓐ Av. del Carmen 24 ⓣ (956) 12 40 44 ⓛ 10.00–23.00

ACCOMMODATION

Arcos de la Frontera

La Casa Grande £–££ Boutique hotel in the old part of town with
a rooftop terrace for relaxing. ⓐ Maldonado 10 ⓣ (956) 70 39 30
ⓦ www.lacasagrande.net

Marqués de Torresoto £–££ A comfortable 17th-century aristocratic house in the old part of town next to the church and the main square. Restaurant on the patio. ⓐ Marqués de Torresoto 4 ⓣ (956) 70 07 17

Grazalema

La Casa de las Piedras £ A converted house in one of the oldest streets in the town. The bedrooms, around a patio, are simply but charmingly furnished and the beds spread with locally made Grazalema blankets. Lounge with fireplace. Six modern apartments further down the street are available for rent. ⓐ C/ de las Piedras 32 ⓣ (956) 13 20 14 ⓦ www.casadelaspiedras.net

△ *Horses graze in an olive grove near Ronda*

Ronda

Arriadh £–££ A five-room hotel with views near Arriate, just outside Ronda. ⓐ Camino de Laura ⓣ (952) 11 43 70 ⓦ www.andalucia.com/arriadh

Alavera de los Baños ££ Homely small hotel next to the Arab baths. Swimming pool. Some rooms have a private terrace. ⓐ Hoyo San Miguel ⓣ (952) 87 91 43 ⓦ www.andalucia.com/alavera

Jardín de la Muralla ££ An elegant country-house hotel to the south of town, with far-reaching views from its garden and pool area, and a cosy lounge filled with books. ⓐ Espiritu Santo 13 ⓣ (952) 87 27 64 ⓦ www.jardindelamuralla.com

Molino del Santo ££ Once a watermill, now a sun-trap with a pleasing swimming pool. 12 km (just over 7 miles) from Ronda. ⓐ Barrada de la Estación, Benaoján ⓣ (952) 16 71 51 ⓦ www.molinodelsanto.com

Reina Victoria ££ Historically, the grand hotel of Ronda – and still retaining some of its elegance and charm. The extensive garden and terrace give great views over the surrounding countryside. ⓐ Jerez 25 ⓣ (952) 87 12 40 ⓦ www.hotelreinavictoriaronda.com

Molino del Arco £££ Family-run guesthouse in a converted olive oil mill. ⓐ Partido de los Frontones, 8 km (5 miles) from Ronda ⓣ (952) 11 40 17 ⓦ www.hotelmolinodelarco.com

Zahara de la Sierra

Marqués de Zahara £ Large old house around a central patio converted into an 11-room hotel and restaurant. ⓐ San Juan 3 ⓣ (956) 12 30 61

Córdoba, Granada & the surrounding towns

Seville is one of the three great cities of Andalucia associated with the medieval Muslim civilisation of Spain. It would be a shame to leave without seeing the other two, Córdoba and Granada. They are easily reached by motorway and have one world-famous monument apiece plus a host of other sights worth visiting. All three cities have very different atmospheres and are, incidentally, packed with bars and restaurants.

Dotted around them are several charming towns that complement the cities – and each other – perfectly.

GETTING THERE

By road

Córdoba is to the northeast of Seville, reachable by road on the N4. There is just one drawback to visiting Córdoba: parking. If you are visiting for the day by car, the best policy is to head for the underground multistorey car park (Ⓐ Av. del Aeropuerto – which, as its name suggests, goes towards the airport), 15 minutes' walk from the monuments. Granada is to the east of Seville, most easily reached by road by taking the N4 to Córdoba, then the N432. The town of Écija is just off the N4 motorway. To drive to Antequera from Seville, take the N4 and N331, and for Osuna, take the N334 and A382.

CÓRDOBA

Roman Córdoba was the capital of southern Spain, but it was after the Muslim invasion of Spain in the 8th century that it truly came into its own. In the 10th and 11th centuries, while the rest of Europe

Córdoba & Granada
City
Large Town
Small Town
Main Road
Minor Road
Railway
Bembézar
Villaviciosa de Córdoba
Tiesa 673
Embalse del Bembézar
CÓRDOBA
Embalse de San Rafael Navallana
Andúja
Linares
Sabiote
Úbeda
Guadalquivir
Guadiana Menor
Madinat al-Zahra
El Carpio
CÓRDOBA
Porcuna
N324
N323
JAÉN
N321
Torre del Campo
JAÉN
Torres
Jódar
Guadajoz
Torreparedones 572
A422
Torredonjimeno
Mágina 2167
Belmez de la Moraleda
Castro del Río
Martos
Guadalquivir
La Victoria
N432
Alcaudete
N323
SEVILLE
N4
Écija
Montilla
Aguilar
Moriles
Cabra
Lobatejo 1380
A333
Alcalá la Real
Almedinilla
Moclín
Puente-Genil
SEVILLA
Lucena
Tiñosa 1570
Javerero 1189
Parapanda 1604
Pinos-Puente
N331
Rute
Embalse de Iznájar
Íllora
Santa Fe
N342
GRANADA
Estepa
N334
A382
Osuna
Becerrero 846
Palenciana
MÁLAGA
Loja
A92
Cabras 1614
GRANADA
Armilla
Córdoba & Granada
0   30 km
0   15 miles
Antequera
Archidona
Cerro de Santa Lucía 1669
Mulhacén 3482
Padul

was wallowing in the dark ages, the civilised place to be was in Muslim Córdoba where Christians and Jews added to a cultural melting pot, and art and learning thrived.

MADINAT AL-ZAHRA

When Muslim Córdoba was at the height of its wealth and power in the 10th century, caliph Abd al-Rahman III decided to build himself a new administrative city-cum-royal residence at the foot of the Sierra Morena that would put medieval Christian Europe to shame. One chronicler speaks of 10,000 men working daily on the vast building site, yet Madinat al-Zahra was to last only 70 years before being sacked in a civil war.

Madinat is the third biggest archaeological dig in Europe after Pompeii and Crete, but only a tenth of its ruins have so far been uncovered. What you see today is a mixture of original remains and reconstruction using modern materials to imitate the originals.

The most interesting part is the Salon de Abd al-Rahman, the only roofed building (towards the bottom of the site), which has arcades of gracious horseshoe arches and rich decoration on its walls and the capitals of columns. ⓐ Madinat is just under 10 km (6 miles) west of Córdoba off the main road towards Palma del Río, well signposted from the city centre ⓣ (957) 32 91 30 ⓦ www.juntadeandalucia.es/cultura/ medinatalzahra ⓛ 10.00–18.30 Tues–Sat, 10.00–14.00 Sun, closed Mon, mid-Sept–Apr; 10.00–20.30 Tues–Sat, closed Sun & Mon, May–mid-Sept

SIGHTS & ATTRACTIONS

The Mesquita

Much of Córdoba's immense attraction derives from its historical religious significance. The magnificence that once typified the city can be seen in the famous *mezquita*, or mosque, that dominates

The Moorish palace at Madinat al-Zahra

the city centre. Built on the site of a Visigothic church, it is the work of four caliphs. What impresses is the immense size of the Hall of Caliph Abd al-Rahman. It is the only building on the site that has a roof, which is supported by over 800 two-tier horseshoe arches rising from slender columns (many of which are recycled from Roman and Visigothic buildings). Because the whole area slopes downhill, you enter from above, and the Hall is near the bottom. On the southern wall is a *mihrab* – prayer niche decorated with intricate plasterwork and mosaics.

When Córdoba was reconquered by the Christians they couldn't leave such a structure untouched to testify to the success of their

▲ *A Moorish patio in Córdoba*

rival religion. Thus, in the 16th century a cathedral was dropped incongruously into the middle of the Hall. The old minaret was simultaneously dressed up as a belfry.

Take a walk around the Judería, the old Jewish quarter of the city near the mosque. This is a delightful jumble of shady alleyways and whitewashed houses decorated with wrought iron grilles and flowerpots. Look out for the *Sinagoga*, synagogue (🕿 (957) 20 29 28), no more than a delightful square hall with richly decorated walls, and one of the only three remaining in Spain. ⓐ Torrijos 🕿 (957) 47 05 12) 🕘 10.00–18.30 Mon–Sat, 13.30–18.30 Sun. Admission charge

RETAIL THERAPY
Zoco Municipal de Artesanía A pretty courtyard close to the synagogue that's occupied by craftsmen and women who can be seen at work in their studios. There's a shop selling their wares as you come in off the street. ⓐ C/ Judios 🕿 (957) 29 05 75 🕘 11.00–14.00, 17.00–20.00 Mon–Fri, 11.00–14.00 Sat, closed Sun

TAKING A BREAK
Bars & cafés
Taberna San Miguel £ Better known as 'El Pisto', a well-known old bar on a bullfighting theme where tapas are served along with Montilla-Moriles wines (the local equivalent of sherry). ⓐ Pl. San Miguel 1 🕿 (957) 47 01 66 🕘 12.00–16.00, 20.00–00.00 Mon–Sat, 12.00–16.00 Sun

AFTER DARK
Restaurants
Casa Pepe de la Judería ££ Tapas downstairs around the patio; restaurant upstairs. ⓐ Romero 1 🕿 (957) 20 07 44 🕘 13.00–16.00, 20.30–23.30

Bodegas Campos £££ Wine *bodega* transformed into a restaurant. A delightful place in itself, but the food is also excellent. ⓐ Lineros 32 ⓣ (957) 49 75 00 ⓦ www.bodegascampos.com ⓛ 13.00–17.00, 20.30–00.00 Mon–Sat, 13.00–17.00 Sun

El Churrasco £££ The city's classic restaurant is dispersed around several patios and other pleasant dining spaces. Specialises in grilled meats. ⓦ http://www.elchurrasco.com ⓛ 13.00–16.00, 20.30–00.00

Flamenco shows

Tablao El Cardenal This venue puts on a flamenco show six nights a week. ⓦ www.tablaocardenal.com ⓛ Shows between 22.30–00.20 Mon–Sat, closed Sun

ACCOMMODATION

Casa de los Naranjos ££ A small hotel with just 20 rooms in the old part of the city. Some of the furnishings were made by local craftsworkers. Internet access available. ⓦ www.casadelosnaranjos.com

Lola ££–£££ Any hotel that dares to advertise itself as 'the most beautiful hotel in Andalucia' must be worth taking a chance on. Each of the eight rooms is individually furnished with a touch of homeliness. Close to the mosque. ⓦ www.hotelconencantolola.com

GRANADA

After a stint as the Roman city of Illibris, Granada passed into Jewish hands before being taken over by Moors. The result is a culturally fascinating city, which, incidentally, is now famous for its buzzing nightlife.

SIGHTS & ATTRACTIONS

The Alhambra

As the last Muslim city of Spain to fall to the Christian reconquest (in 1492), Granada had time to see its civilisation mature before being eclipsed. The result is the Alhambra, an exquisite palace-fortress that sits on a hill above the city. The complex is made up of three parts: the fortress or Alcazaba, the summer palace of the Generalife (of interest mainly for its gardens) and the Royal or

![The mountains of the Sierra Nevada soar above the Alhambra at Granada]

The mountains of the Sierra Nevada soar above the Alhambra at Granada

Nazrid Palace. This last part, an exquisite assembly of patios and intricately decorated halls mostly built in the 14th century, is what everyone comes to see. Visitor numbers are restricted and it is essential to book ahead. ❶ (902) 22 44 60 Ⓦ www.alhambra.org ❶ 08.30–18.00 Nov–Feb; 08.30–20.00 Mar–Oct

Capilla Real

This exquisite, Gothic royal funerary chapel, which houses the remains of several Spanish kings, is a great place to come for some peace in the middle of the city. Its many decorative features include stunning baroque sculptures. ⓐ Oficios 3 ❶ (958) 22 92 39 Ⓦ www.capillarealgranada.com ❶ 10.30–13.00, 15.30–18.00 Mon–Sat, 11.00–13.30, 15.30–18.00 Sun. Admission charge

Corral del Carbón

This 600-year-old building has a fascinating history: once a Moorish B&B, then a Christian theatre, it's now a *bona fide* tourist draw. ⓐ Puente Carbón 2 ❶ (958) 227 697 ❶ 09.00–20.00 Mon–Fri, 10.00–19.00 Sat, 10.00–15.00 Sun

RETAIL THERAPY

Alcaicería Granada's 'Arab market' next to the cathedral has become one large gift-shop selling typical Andalucian souvenirs. However, there are a few craft shops of quality such as Artesanía Alcaicería (nos 1, 3 and 10), which specialises in miniature figures for Christmas cribs. ❶ (958) 22 90 45 Ⓦ www.alcaiceria.com ❶ 10.00–20.00

TAKING A BREAK

Granada is one of the few places in Spain where bars serve a complimentary tapas with each drink – although you can't, of course, choose what you get. Hopping around the bars that serve the best tapas – some old favourites, some recently opened – is a popular way to start an evening. You can tell which places serve the best tapas of the moment because the crowds make it difficult to get through the door let alone to the bar. Good places to hunt for authentic tapas bars include the streets around Plaza Nueva and the streets around Campo del Principe. Four long-established and highly rated tapas bars are as follows.

Bodega Espadafor £ An old-fashioned bar, well known for its tapas. ⓐ Tinajilla ⓣ (958) 20 21 38 ⓛ 12.00–16.00, 20.00–00.00 Mon–Sat, closed Sun, June–Sept; 12.00–16.00, 20.00–00.00 Tues–Sun, closed Mon, Oct–May

Bodegas Castañeda £ Near Plaza Nueva. Gets crowded. ⓐ Almireceros 1–3 ⓣ (958) 21 54 64 ⓛ 11.30–16.30, 19.30–01.00 Mon–Thur, 11.30–01.00 Fri–Sun

Casa Enrique £ Good choice of wines as well as excellent tapas. ⓐ Acerca del Darro 8 ⓣ (958) 25 50 08 ⓛ 12.00–16.00, 20.00–00.00 Mon–Sat, closed Sun

Los Diamantes £ Specialises in fish and seafood. ⓐ Navas 26 ⓣ (958) 22 70 70 ⓛ 13.00–16.00, 20.00–22.30 Mon–Fri, closed Sat & Sun

AFTER DARK

Granada-10 A cinema in the evening which becomes a disco at night, playing disco, hip hop, funk, Latin, salsa – you name it. ⓐ Carc'él Baja 10 ⓣ (958) 22 40 01 ⓦ www.hostalmeridiano.com

ACCOMMODATION

Casa de Federico ££ A small hotel near the cathedral in which the interior design is a striking and harmonious combination of old and new materials. ⓐ Horno de Marina 13 ⓣ (958) 20 85 34 ⓦ www.casadefederico.com

Alhambra Palace £££ A glorious mock-Mooorish building on the same hillside as the Alhambra and with great views from its bar-terrace (open to the public). ⓐ Plaza Arquitecto García de Paredes 1 ⓣ (958) 22 14 68 ⓦ www.h-alhambrapalace.es

Palacio de los Patos £££ Recently voted 'Best Hotel in Europe', this is a swish boutique hotel with garden and spa from the Hospes group. ⓐ Solarillo de Gracia 1 ⓣ (958) 53 65 16 ⓦ www.hospes.es

Parador de San Francisco £££ One of the most luxurious hotels in the state-run chain, in a historic building in an incomparable setting beside the Alhambra. It's essential to reserve as far ahead as possible, as it quickly gets booked up. ⓐ Real de la Alhambra ⓣ (958) 22 14 40 ⓦ www.parador.es

THE SURROUNDING TOWNS

Antequera

This ancient town at the crossroads between Seville, Granada, Malaga and Córdoba has two clusters of monuments. One is uphill from the tourist information office through a formal 16th-century gateway, the Arco de los Gigantes (Giants' Arch), and includes the Renaissance church of Real Colegiata de Santa María la Mayor and the remains of a Muslim fortress, the Alcazaba.

Far older than anything else you will see in Andalucia are three impressive *dólmenes* (dolmens, Neolithic stone formations) on the edge of town. The largest is the Dólmen de Menga, dating, like its neighbour the Dólmen de Viera, from 2500 BC. However, the most interesting is the Dólmen de Romeral because of its domed chamber – the first case of intentional architectural construction in Europe.

Tourist information ⓐ Pl. San Sebastían 7 ❶ (952) 70 81 42 or 70 25 05 ⓦ www.antequera.es ❶ 11.00–14.00, 17.00–20.00 Mon–Sat, 11.00–14.00 Sun

Dólmenes de Viera, Menga & Romeral ⓐ On the road out towards Archidona ❶ 09.00–18.00 Tues–Sat, 09.30–14.30 Sun, closed Mon

Écija

Écija makes a useful stopover on the way to or from Córdoba. Its main attractions are its 11 churches' baroque steeples. All the main sights can be reached on foot from the main square, the Plaza de España.

Tourist information ⓐ www.turismoecija.com ❶ 09.30–15.00 Mon–Fri, 10.30–13.30 Sat & Sun

Osuna

Although not very significant today, in the 16th century Osuna was bequeathed a cluster of monumental buildings by the dukes who took their title from it. To explore the most interesting part, head upwards from the Plaza Mayor towards the Renaissance church, which overlooks the town. Down below there is an archaeological museum, the **Museo Arquelógico** (ⓐ Pl. de la Duquesa ❶ (954) 81 12 07, ❶ 10.00–13.30, 15.30–18.30 Tues–Sun, Nov–Apr; 10.00–13.30, 16.00–19.00 Tues–Sun, May–Jun & Oct; 10.00–13.30, 16.00–19.00 Tues–Sat,

10.00–13.30 Sun, Jul & Aug; closed Mon), in one of the town's most ancient buildings, the 12th-century Torre del Agua.
Tourist information ⓐ Pl. Mayor ❶ (954) 81 57 32 ⓦ www.ayto-osuna.es ❶ 09.00–14.00, 16.00–18.00 Mon–Fri, closed Sat & Sun

TAKING A BREAK

Casa Curro £ A bar with a good selection of tapas. ⓐ Pl. Salitre 5, Osuna ❶ (955) 82 07 58 ❶ 12.00–00.30 Tues–Sun, closed Mon

AFTER DARK

Caserío de San Benito ££ This very traditional and much-loved restaurant lies a few miles north of Antequera, in the direction of Cordoba. ⓐ Carretera Córdoba–Málaga km 108, Antequera ❶ (952) 11 11 03 ⓦ www.caseriodesanbenito.com ❶ 20.00–00.00 Fri–Sun, closed Mon–Thur

ACCOMMODATION

Palacio de los Granados £££ Boutique hotel in a baroque mansion with a small pool in the courtyard. Tapas or a full dinner (on request) served in the evening. ⓐ Emilio Castelar 42, Écija ❶ (955) 90 10 50 ⓦ www.palaciogranados.com

Palacio Marqués de la Gomera £££ Small hotel in an 18th-century aristocratic mansion with a renowned restaurant, La Casa del Marqués. ⓐ San Pedro 20, Osuna ❶ (954) 81 22 23 ⓦ www.hotelpalaciodelmarques.com

◗ *A blue tram glides past Seville's cathedral*

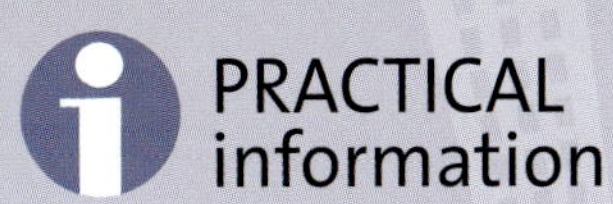

PRACTICAL
information

Directory

GETTING THERE

By air

Seville's Aeropuerto de San Pablo (see page 48), located 12 km (7$^1/_2$ miles) east of the city, is served by a number of scheduled international airlines, four of them flying in from UK airports. Flying time from Britain is around 2$^1/_2$ hours. For details of getting from the airport to the city centre, see page 48.

Iberia Spain's national airline flies from London Heathrow, most European and many other major airports. It, or its subsidiaries, operate domestic flights within Spain ❶ (902) 40 05 00; in UK 0870 609 050 Ⓦ www.iberia.com

For Iberia's office in Seville contact ⓐ Av. de la Buhaira 8 (Cecofar building) ❶ (954) 98 82 08 Ⓦ www.iberia.es

Iberia's new low-cost arm, **Click Air**, also flies from Heathrow to Seville ❶ (from UK) 0800 254 25247; (from Spain) (902) 25 42 52 Ⓦ www.clickair.es

British Airways (operated by franchisee **GB Airways**) flies from London Gatwick ❶ (902) 11 13 33; in UK 0870 850 98 50 Ⓦ www.britishairways.com

Ryanair flies from London Stansted and Liverpool to Seville ❶ (954) 44 92 32; in UK 0871 246 0000 Ⓦ www.ryanair.com

Air Berlin flies from London Stansted to Seville ❶ (954) 26 07 03; in UK 0870 738 88 80 Ⓦ www.airberlin.com

Visitors from the USA and other continents may either fly directly to Seville or take a connecting flight from most major European airports. Visitors from elsewhere in Europe should travel via their nearest major city, all of which have plane connections to Seville.

Many people are aware that air travel emits CO_2, which contributes to climate change. You may be interested in the possibility of lessening the environmental impact of your flight through the charity Climate Care, which offsets your CO_2 by funding environmental projects around the world Ⓦ www.climatecare.org

By rail

Seville's main railway station is Estación Santa Justa (see page 48).

Mainline and local trains are operated by the national company RENFE (Red Nacional de Ferrocarriles Españoles). Full details of these services can be obtained from Ⓣ (902) 24 02 02 or Ⓦ www.renfe.es

The journey time from Madrid on board the high speed AVE (Alta Velocidad Española) train is 2½ hours.

To plan a rail trip from the UK to Spain, it's best to go through an international agent such as **Rail Europe** (Ⓐ 1 Regent Street, London SW1Y 4NR Ⓣ (0844) 848 40 64 Ⓦ www.raileurope.co.uk Ⓝ Piccadilly Circus). Ⓘ It takes about two days non-stop to get to Seville from London by rail

By road

From any of the French Channel ports, head south to Biarritz and cross the frontier at the western end of the Pyrenees (between Hendaye and Irún) to reach San Sebastian. Turn inland for Vitoria-Gasteiz and pick up the N-I motorway for Madrid at Burgos.

Madrid's orbital motorways take some navigating. Arriving from the north there is no sign saying Seville. The best policy is to go around Madrid to the east on the M40 following signs first for Zaragoza (but don't turn off for that city), then Valencia, then Córdoba. If you're lucky, you'll find yourself heading due south on the N4 motorway through La Mancha (past Aranjuez) and eventually through the spectacular pass of Despeñaperros into Andalucia. Follow the signs for Córdoba and then keep on the same motorway for Seville.

Alternatively, to save driving through France, take a ferry to Bilbao or Santander (crossing 24–30 hours), and drive south to Burgos, then on to Madrid.

Driving around the centre of Seville may take some getting used to and is best avoided in favour of walking and public transport. Parking can be both difficult and expensive. What's more, some people choose to double park which makes the traffic problem worse.

Spain drives on the right and its highway code is similar to that of other European countries, with internationally recognisable traffic signs. The police can issue on-the-spot fines for traffic offences and being a foreigner does not give you exemption. Seat belts are obligatory and children under 12 should travel in the back.

Speed limits are 120 km/h (74 mph) on motorways, 100 km/h (62 mph) on roads and 50 km/h (31 mph) in built-up areas.

Petrol (*gasolina*) is available as *super*, *normal* (both leaded), *sin plomo* (unleaded) and *gasoil* (diesel).

SOME WARNINGS ABOUT DRIVING

- It is forbidden to drive under the influence of alcohol.
- Most national driving licences are valid, but it is advisable to have an international driving licence.
- In your car you must carry a red warning triangle, replacement light bulbs and a reflective jacket in the passenger compartment to wear in case of emergency.
- If you wear glasses, you must have a spare pair in the car.

All the major car-hire companies have offices in Seville (see page 58). Rates are competitive, but you can usually get the best deal by reserving a car from home at the same time as making a flight booking. ❶ When hiring a car you will be asked to show your passport and an EU or international driving licence, as well as a credit (not debit) card

ENTRY FORMALITIES

Most visitors – including citizens of all EU countries, the USA, Canada, Ireland, Australia and New Zealand – require only a valid passport to enter Spain. Visitors from South Africa must have a visa. There is no restriction on what items you may bring in with you as a tourist, but you'll find almost everything you need locally. In Spain you are obliged by law to carry your passport with you all the time in case the police ask for identification.

MONEY

The Spanish currency is the euro. It is divided into 100 cents or céntimos. There are coins of 1 and 2 euros, and of 1, 2, 5, 10, 20 and 50 cents. The notes are in denominations of 5, 10, 20, 50, 100, 200 and 500 euros. Banks are generally open only in the morning from 09.00–13.30 Mon–Fri, but there are many cash machines in Seville where you can obtain money with a credit card. Credit cards are accepted for payment almost everywhere except in smaller bars, shops and *pensiones*. Traveller's cheques can be cashed in banks and big hotels. Personal cheques are not accepted anywhere.

HEALTH, SAFETY & CRIME

Although EU citizenship gives you basic health cover in Spain on production of a European Health Insurance Card (EHIC, available on-line at Ⓦ www.ehic.org.uk), it is advisable to take out personal travel insurance as well. This can be obtained from your travel agent, airline company or any insurance company. Make sure it gives adequate cover not only for medical expenses but also for loss or theft of possessions, personal liability and repatriation in an emergency.

If you are going to Spain by car, ask your insurer for a green card and check with them on the cover you will need for damage, loss or theft of the vehicle and for legal costs in the event of an accident.

If you hire a car you will be asked whether you want to pay extra for collision insurance. You may already be covered for this by your normal UK car insurance.

A mobile police presence makes for a safer city

Like any big city, Seville has its share of petty crime. That said, most of it is opportunist and a few simple precautions will make sure you are not an easy target.

- Watch out for pickpockets in crowed places like markets and bars, and keep your bag across your chest and in front of you.
- Leave valuables in a hotel safe, and never leave anything on display in a parked car.

OPENING HOURS

Shops Usual opening hours are 09.00 or 10.00–13.30 & 17.00–20.30 Mon–Sat. In the summer, some shops open later in the afternoon when the heat starts to die down and stay open correspondingly later. Department stores and other large shops open continuously 10.00–21.00. Shops are generally closed on Sundays except on special occasions such as the run up to Christmas.

Post offices These are generally open 09.00–14.00 Mon–Fri & 09.00–13.00 Sat.

Banks These are usually open from 09.00–13.30 Mon–Fri.

Offices (government and private business) These are generally open 09.00–14.00 & 16.00–20.00 Mon–Fri. In summer, many offices work a reduced day from 08.00–15.00, then close until the next morning.

Museums Opening hours are generally 09.00–13.00 & 16.00–20.00 Tues–Sat and perhaps Sun morning. They usually close on Mondays, although there are exceptions.

Restaurants Mealtimes in Spain are later than in the rest of Europe. Breakfast in hotels is served 07.30–10.00; lunch is 14.00–16.00; and dinner is generally 21.00–23.00.

Entertainment Larger cinemas have several showings a day from 16.00–23.00. Some theatres offer two daily performances at 18.00

& 22.00. Bars for drinking and musical venues are open 21.00–03.00 and discos 11.30–05.00 or 06.00.

If you are making a special journey to a museum, restaurant, etc., always check precise opening times before you set out.

TOILETS

Seville has few public toilets. The most convenient thing to do, therefore, is go into a bar or café – in which case it is polite to buy a drink. Another option is to use those in a department store like El Corte Inglés (see page 69). There are several Spanish words for 'toilets', the most common being *servicios*, *aseos* and *lavabos*.

CHILDREN

In Spain children simply fit into ordinary life. There may not be many special facilities for them, but this lack is more than made up for by a general tolerance and willingness to help. For instance, you are unlikely to see a 'child menu', but you are also unlikely to come across a waiter who won't go out of his way to make sure a child gets something suitable to eat.

If you fancy a nice family outing, try a mooch around the Isla Mágica theme park (see page 95). Most children like (to them) quaint forms of transport, and so a river-boat trip (see page 55) or a horse and carriage ride (see page 58) should go down well. If your children are animal fans, head for the best zoo in the region, the **Zoo Botánico** in Jerez (C/ Taxdirt, Jeréz de la Frontera (956) 15 34 61). And if all the family feels like some smashing splashing in a cool pool, dive over to **Aquopolis Seville** water park (Av. del Deporte, near the Palacio de Congresos, east of the city centre (954) 40 66 22 www.aquopolis.es/sevilla).

The kids will love a trip to the 'Magic Island' theme park

COMMUNICATIONS

Internet

Seville is as wired as you'd expect any major European city to be, and three of the best *cafés cibernéticos* (internet cafés) are:

Amazonas Cyber ⓐ Conde de Barajas 6 ⓦ www.amazonascyber.com

Sevilla Internet Center ⓐ Almirantzago 2–10
ⓦ www.sevilleinternetcenter.com

ADS ⓐ San Luis 108 (near Macarena basilica)

Phone

Local, national and international calls can all be made from *cabinas* (public phone booths) in the street, which operate with coins or cards. Instructions are written in several languages. Some call boxes also take credit cards. *Tarjetas telefónicas* (phonecards) are on sale at *estancos* (tobacconists) and *correos* (post offices).

You can also phone from *locutorios*, public telephone centres which are quieter and more convenient than phone boxes. Pay at the counter when you have finished your call.

Calls from a hotel room are more expensive than from phone boxes or *locutorios*.

Post

Correos (post offices) are open 08.00–21.00 Mon–Fri & 09.00–14.00 Sat. The main post office is at ⓐ Av. de la Constitución 32 ⓣ (902) 19 71 97. If you just want stamps don't bother to look for a post office; buy them in an *estanco* (tobacconists). The cost to send a card or letter up to 20 g is 0.57 cents to a country within the EU and 0.78 cents to the rest of the world. After that, prices vary according to weight. Post boxes are yellow.

❶ To send a telegram ⓣ (902) 19 71 97

TELEPHONING SPAIN

To call Spain from abroad, dial the international access code (often 00) + the country code (34) + the phone number (including the provincial/area code), omitting the initial zero.

TELEPHONING ABROAD

To call abroad from Spain, dial 00 + the country code + the phone number, omitting the initial zero. The country code for the UK is 44, for Ireland 353, for the USA and Canada 1, for Australia 61, for New Zealand 64 and for South Africa 27.
For international information call ☎ 11825
For national information call ☎ 11818
You can also find phone numbers at ⓦ www.paginasamarillas.es (the Spanish yellow pages) and ⓦ www.paginasblancas.es (the normal phone book listing subscribers).
For any other information on telephoning in Spain see the website of the national phone company, **Telefonica** ⓦ www.telefonica.es

ELECTRICITY

Spain's electricity supply is 220 volt, but you may find an anachronistic 125-volt outlet occasionally in an older building, and for sensitive appliances like computers and mobile phones it is worth double checking the voltage before plugging them in.
❶ All plugs in Spain have two round pins, so electrical devices from the UK will only work with an adapter. Visitors from North America will need a transformer.

TRAVELLERS WITH DISABILITIES

Spain doesn't have many facilities for travellers with disabilities, but the situation is slowly changing. More information is available from:

COCEMFE ⓐ Luis Cabrera 63, Madrid ⓣ (917) 44 36 00 ⓦ www.cocemfe.es

RADAR (The Royal Association for Disability and Rehabilitation) ⓣ 020 7250 3222 ⓦ www.radar.org.uk

Holiday Care Service ⓣ 0845 124 99 71 ⓦ www.holidaycare.org.uk

TOURIST INFORMATION

Before travelling to Spain, general information about the country can be obtained from the Spanish Tourist Office in London (ⓣ 020 7486 8077 ⓛ 09.15–13.30 Mon–Fri ⓘ Visits are strictly by appointment).

Basic questions can be answered by visiting ⓦ www.tourspain.co.uk and ⓦ www.tourspain.es

The main tourist office in Seville (ⓐ Pl. de San Francisco 19 ⓣ (954) 59 52 88) is next to the town hall and the official website for Seville is ⓦ www.turismo.sevilla.org

There are also tourist information offices at the airport (ⓣ (954) 44 91 28) and Santa Justa Station (ⓣ (954) 53 76 26).

The tourist office for Andalucia in Seville province (including Itálica and Carmona) is at ⓐ Pl. del Triunfo 1–3 ⓣ (954) 50 10 01

For information about other places in Andalucia – including Jerez, the white towns, Doñana National Park, Córdoba and Granada – contact the Junta de Andalucia's office (ⓐ Av. de la Constitución 21B ⓣ (954) 22 14 04 ⓦ www.andalucia.org).

Andalucia's tourist helpline is ⓣ (901) 20 00 20

COMPLAINTS

Spain has strong consumer laws and a strict order in which to make a complaint. First, explain to the establishment in question why you are unhappy with its product or service. This will usually get results, but if it doesn't your next course of action is to fill in a *hoja de reclamaciones* (official complaints form). That will set in motion an official investigation, but if you want to see what other options you have, contact Seville's **OMIC** (Municipal Consumer Information Office ⓐ Av. Portugal 2 ⓣ (954) 23 18 22). If you are still not satisfied, you can apply to the **European Consumer Centre** (ⓐ Principe Vergara 54, 28006 Madrid ⓣ (918) 22 45 55 ⓦ cec.consumo-inc.es).

BACKGROUND READING

Andalucía by Michael Jacobs. If you only read one other book on southern Spain, make it this one.

The Seville Communion by Arturo Perez Reverte. A novel that conveys the flavour of the city in which it is set.

The New Spaniards by John Hooper. For background on contemporary Spain, this is a thorough and readable account of social and political change since the death of Franco.

Emergencies

The following are the separate emergency numbers for police, fire and ambulance (but, if in doubt, use the general emergency number 112 to get you through to the service you need):

General emergencies 112   **Fire brigade** 080
Policía Nacional 091   **Policía Municipal** 092

MEDICAL SERVICES
Ambulances & hospitals
To summon an ambulance 112
Hospital Universitario Virgen Macarena Av. Dr Fedriani
(955) 00 80 00 (English-speaking doctors available)
Hospital Virgen del Rocío Av. Manuel Siurot (955) 01 20 00
Hospital Virgen de Valme Av. Ctra. Sevilla-Cádiz (955) 01 50 00

Pharmacies
Minor health problems can often be cleared up by consulting a *farmacia*, a chemist's shop that is indicated by a green cross sign. Out of hours, there is always one *farmacia de guardia* open. You'll find its address posted in the window of other *farmacias*.

POLICE
Seville has three police forces. The Policía Municipal is responsible for traffic problems and low-level policing. The Policía Nacional is in charge of more serious crime. The Guardia Civil takes care of highway patrols and customs.

Contact the police for information on (900) 15 00 00 or to make a complaint on (902) 10 21 12 www.policia.es

Main police station Av. Blas Infante 2 (954) 28 93 00

If you leave an item on a plane, bus or train, contact the company in question and see if it has been handed in. Report the loss of valuable items to a police station. You will need an official form to make an insurance claim.

EMBASSIES & CONSULATES

Australia ⓐ Federico Rubio 14 ⓣ (954) 22 09 71 ⓦ www.embaustralia.es

Canada ⓐ Málaga: Pl. Malagueta 3 ⓣ (952) 22 33 46 ⓦ www.canada-es.org

Ireland ⓐ Pl. de Santa Cruz 6 ⓣ (954) 21 63 61

New Zealand ⓐ Embassy in Madrid: 3rd floor, Pl. de la Lealtad 2 ⓣ (915) 23 02 26

South Africa ⓐ Embassy in Madrid. Claudio Coello 91 ⓣ (914) 36 37 80

UK ⓐ Tomares: Urb. Aljamar, block 7 no. 145 ⓣ (954) 15 50 18 ⓦ www.ukinspain.com

US ⓐ Pl. Nueva 8 ⓣ (954) 21 85 71 ⓦ www.embusa.es

EMERGENCY PHRASES

Help!	**Fire!**	**Stop!**
¡Socorro!	¡Fuego!	¡Stop!
¡Sawkoro!	*¡Fwegoh!*	*¡Stop!*

Call an ambulance/a doctor/the police/the fire service!
¡Llame a una ambulancia/un médico/la policía/a los bomberos!
¡Lliame a oona anboolanthea/oon meydico/la poletheea/
a lohs bombehrohs!

WHAT'S IN YOUR GUIDEBOOK?

Independent authors Impartial up-to-date information from our travel experts who meticulously source local knowledge.

Experience Thomas Cook's 165 years in the travel industry and guidebook publishing enriches every word with expertise you can trust.

Travel know-how Contributions by thousands of staff around the globe, each one living and breathing travel.

Editors Travel-publishing professionals, pulling everything together to craft a perfect blend of words, pictures, maps and design.

You, the traveller We deliver a practical, no-nonsense approach to information, geared to how you really use it.

SPOTTED YOUR NEXT CITY BREAK?

Then these lightweight CitySpots pocket guides will have you in the know in no time, wherever you're heading. Covering over 80 cities worldwide, they're packed with detail on the most important urban attractions from shopping and sights to non-stop nightlife; knocking spots off chunkier, clunkier versions.

Aarhus	Genoa	Paris
Amsterdam	Glasgow	Prague
Antwerp	Gothenburg	Porto
Athens	Granada	Reykjavik
Bangkok	Hamburg	Riga
Barcelona	Hanover	Rome
Belfast	Helsinki	Rotterdam
Belgrade	Hong Kong	Salzburg
Berlin	Istanbul	Sarajevo
Bilbao	Kiev	Seville
Bologna	Krakow	Singapore
Bordeaux	Kuala Lumpur	Sofia
Bratislava	Leipzig	Stockholm
Bruges	Lille	Strasbourg
Brussels	Lisbon	St Petersburg
Bucharest	Ljubljana	Tallinn
Budapest	London	Tirana
Cairo	Los Angeles	Tokyo
Cape Town	Lyon	Toulouse
Cardiff	Madrid	Turin
Cologne	Marrakech	Valencia
Copenhagen	Marseilles	Venice
Cork	Milan	Verona
Dubai	Monte Carlo	Vienna
Dublin	Moscow	Vilnius
Dubrovnik	Munich	Warsaw
Düsseldorf	Naples	Zagreb
Edinburgh	New York	Zurich
Florence	Nice	
Frankfurt	Oslo	
Gdansk	Palermo	
Geneva	Palma	

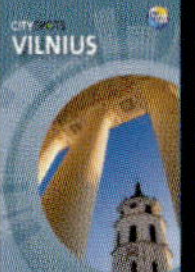

Available from all good bookshops, your local Thomas Cook travel store or browse and buy on-line at www.thomascookpublishing.com

Thomas Cook
Publishing

Editorial/project management: Lisa Plumridge with Laetitia Clapton
Copy editor: Paul Hines
Layout/DTP: Pat Hinsley & Alison Rayner
Proofreader: Wendy Janes

The publishers would like to thank the following individuals and organisations for supplying copyright photographs for this book: Dreamstime.com (Michael Corrigan, page 80; Francisco Javier Alcerreca Gomez, page 13; Jarnogz, page 64; Lorenzo Lesca, pages 40–1; Graça Victoria, page 59); Francisco Javier Alcerreca Gomez/BigStockPhoto.com, page 10; iStockphoto.com (Graham Heywood, page 141; Stephan Hoerold, page 146; Hani Alex Latif, page 9; Roberto A Sanchez, page 89); Alex Lapuerta Mediavilla/123RF, page 101; Pictures Colour Library, pages 103, 122 & 135; SXC.hu (Sue Anna Joe, page 70; Carlos Zaragoza, page 1); Turespana, pages 5 & 7; Nick Inman, all others.

Send your thoughts to
books@thomascook.com

- **Found a great bar, club, shop or must-see sight that we don't feature?**
- **Like to tip us off about any information that needs a little updating?**
- **Want to tell us what you love about this handy little guidebook and more importantly how we can make it even handier?**

Then here's your chance to tell all! Send us ideas, discoveries and recommendations today and then look out for your valuable input in the next edition of this title.

Email the above address (stating the title) or write to:
CitySpots Project Editor, Thomas Cook Publishing, PO Box 227, Coningsby Road, Peterborough PE3 8SB, UK.